STUDIES IN AFRICAN HISTORY · 6

Ghana under Military Rule
1966-1969

ROBERT PINKNEY

GHANA UNDER MILITARY RULE 1966–1969

METHUEN & CO LTD
11 New Fetter Lane · London EC4

First published 1972 by Methuen & Co Ltd
© *1972 Robert Pinkney*
Printed in Great Britain by
Richard Clay (The Chaucer Press) Ltd
Bungay, Suffolk

SBN 416 75080 X   hardback
SBN 416 75090 7   paperback

Distributed in the USA
by HARPER & ROW PUBLISHERS, INC.
BARNES & NOBLE IMPORT DIVISION

Contents

Introduction

This is a case study of the operation of a military government. Writers on such governments have suggested that once the shooting has stopped, the men who have taken power are faced with certain common problems and that in attempting to tackle these, they possess both assets and weaknesses in comparison with their counterparts who head civilian administrations. The problems include deciding clearly what to do with power once it has been seized; the establishment of legitimacy in the eyes of those both at home and abroad; securing public co-operation (or at least preventing non-co-operation); deciding the ways in which civilians should be employed within the political process, and either ensuring the orderly transfer of power to a friendly civilian government or finding an acceptable way of perpetuating military rule. The assets such rulers usually possess include the goodwill of those dissatisfied, often for conflicting reasons, with the previous regime, a reputation untarnished by political intrigue, in government or opposition, a 'national' reputation which transcends sectional groupings, and control of the weapons of coercion. In the case of Ghana, the presence of the police in the Government, with their extensive intelligence services and their greater experience of handling civilians, provided additional assets. (The term 'military rule' is used throughout for the sake of brevity, but, unless otherwise indicated, it is used to cover the police as well as the army.)

The weaknesses are more difficult to pinpoint. They are usually said to include, to a greater or lesser degree, lack of a 'popular base', a lack of clearly worked out political objectives and little skill in ensuring the execution of such policies as the rulers do choose. Given sufficient time in a position of power, soldiers and policemen may acquire some of both the vices and virtues of politicians, and the course of political change may depend on which are acquired more rapidly. The vices include corruption, the acquisition of personal fortunes and failure to fulfil promises, all of which provide moral ammunition for anyone plotting a counter-coup. The virtues include a willingness to listen to public opinion and ability to conciliate sections of it, and a greater understanding of what can or cannot be achieved through the skilled manipulation of the levers of power, particularly in relation to the Civil Service and consultative bodies.

The study of the three and a half years of military rule in Ghana will be considered against this background of problems, assets and weaknesses. After examining the objectives of those who took power in February 1966, consideration will be given to their attitude to public opinion, the way in which they handled the Civil Service, the extent of dependence on civilians from outside the service and the processes by which civilian rule was restored. The chapter on regional administration is included because the majority of 'political demands' in Ghana are for the provision or improvement of local amenities, and the chapter should help to avoid the impression that political interest during this period centred solely around issues such as what sort of agreements should be signed with foreign firms, or how many industries should be denationalized.

It is hoped that this case study will advance the study of the involvement of the military in politics by testing some of the broad generalizations that have been made on the subject. The study indicates that, while some of the events in Ghana between 1966 and 1969 were directly attributable to the fact that the Government was a military one, the similarities between uniformed officers and the most influential sections of the civilian population were as striking as the differences. In the case of Ghana, there is little evidence to support the widely held view that military men bring into politics distinctive values or styles of government. If the officers' mess helped to shape political views, so too did institutions and experiences common to both uniformed men and many civilians, including the extended family, the mission school and life under colonial and presidential rule.

Ghana was originally chosen for this study in preference to any other African state because I had worked there in the early days of the First Republic. The choice proved a fortunate one in the sense that there was a favourable research climate when I returned to Ghana eight years later. It was possible to interview over ninety people, including the majority of members of the National Executive Council, the Political Committee, and the National Advisory Committee, together with several chiefs, pressure-group leaders and civil servants in nearly all the ministries and regional offices. The choice also proved to be a rewarding one in that Ghana provided an example, rare so far in Africa, of a military government keeping to the timetable it had set itself for restoring civilian rule.

Much of the research was carried out at the Ghana High Commission in London and the British Museum Newspaper Library, and the interviews conducted in Ghana provided an invaluable source of information. These were important in revealing not only the facts, but also the wide variety of perceptions of the ways in which different individuals and institutions involved in Ghanaian politics functioned.

Many people and institutions made the completion of the book possible. The London Borough of Hounslow released me from some of my teaching duties at Isleworth Polytechnic to enable me to carry out the research; the University of London Central Research Fund and the Nuffield Foundation financed my fieldwork during 1969 and 1970. While I was in Ghana, I benefited from the guidance of Dr Eric Ayisi, Mr Joe Peasah, and Mr Yaw Twumasi of the University of Ghana. It was largely due to Dr Ayisi's knowledge of, and extensive range of contacts in, Ghanaian politics that I was able to meet so many people. The ninety interviewees are not quoted in the text by name, but I would like to acknowledge the help given by Mr E. C. Quist-Therson and Mr B. A. Yakubu in permitting me to meet many members of the Civil Service and the police force. Most of the people with whom I requested interviews were generous in giving me the benefit of their time and knowledge. In London, I found the staff of the Ghana High Commission equally helpful in dealing with my inquiries.

The subject was originally suggested by Professor Dennis Austin of the University of Manchester. Throughout every stage of my research, the constant criticism and advice of Mr Peter Dawson of the London School of Economics was invaluable. The manuscript was typed by my mother, and by Mrs E. Bedford, Miss J. Campion and Mrs F. N. McColgan. It was read by Mr James Nti of the Institute of Public Administration, Achimota, who made several helpful suggestions.

To all those who have helped in these different ways, I am very grateful. The opinions expressed in the book, and any errors that remain, are my responsibility alone.

1 · Expectations

The starting point of this study is the morning of 24 February 1966. Much has already been written on the Government in power in Ghana until that morning, and on the reasons why it was overthrown.[1] This chapter is concerned with the picture the army and police officers who overthrew President Nkrumah had of the sort of Ghana that would emerge as a result of military rule.

When a change of Government is brought about by force of arms, those bringing about the change have not normally had the time, or the courage, to draft a manifesto. All their energies are devoted to ensuring the successful acquisition of power, and decisions as to what to do with that power are among the least urgent considerations. This was the case in Ghana in February 1966. The army and police shared with many sections of Ghana's civilian population a dislike of President Nkrumah's policies which, they felt, had led to arbitrary imprisonment, the suppression of freedom of expression, economic hardship and widespread corruption. They also had their own specific grievances resulting largely from Dr Nkrumah's creation of his own personal army and security system. These grievances came out clearly in the pronouncements of the new Government once it had gained power.

The broadcast announcing the seizure of power gave the reasons as chaotic economic conditions; the concentration of power in the hands of one man, leading to the abuse of individual rights and liberties, and the capricious exercise of power by the former President, who was said to have run the country as if it were his own personal property.[2] Charges of corruption only came later when people were able to give evidence to the commissions of inquiry set up by the new Government. Writing a book on the *coup d'état* some months after it had occurred, General Afrifa, one of its principal architects, devoted a chapter to the plight of the Ghanaian soldier, in which he described the better pay and equipment enjoyed by the President's Own Guard Regiment in comparison with the regular army, and the way in which Major General Otu, the most senior officer, was often by-passed by his subordinates in advising the president. The dismissal of Generals Ankrah and Otu was said to be a 'major reason' for the coup.[3] (All the army officers who served in the military Government from the start eventually reached the rank of major-general or lieutenant-general. They will be referred to by the rank of 'general' throughout this book irrespective of the ranks they held at particular times.) General Ocran's memoirs were published nearly three years later and he, too, devoted much attention to Dr Nkrumah's treatment of the regular army. One chapter concentrated on the privileges of the President's Own Guard Regiment,[4] and another was concerned with the plight of the regular army:

> One day they were to pay for their electricity; the next day they were to lose their training allowances; the following day they were to lose their travelling facilities. We all wondered what was happening to us.[5]

> The commanders were hard put to it. They had known and been accustomed to a high standard of turnout and cleanliness. What, then, could they do to soldiers who turned out on parade in torn uniforms, with the underwear showing underneath their shorts or trousers? Soldiers with no polish or shine on their boots or with their toes showing through their canvas shoes?[6]

> By late 1965, the going was getting tough for most senior officers. The salaries introduced in 1957 meant little in 1965. They were worth only a third of their value.[7]

It is difficult to assess how far the coup was due to the internal grievances of the army and police, and how far it was due to dislike of Dr Nkrumah's policies as a whole. Many of the grievances of uniformed men were common to many sections of the community. Private soldiers were not the only people wearing tattered clothes, and their officers were not the only people whose salaries had been affected by inflation. The army and police were not the only institutions that disliked what they regarded as 'presidential interference'. The presidential shadow was cast not only over them, but over Parliament, the ruling party, the Civil Service, the trade unions and the Young Pioneers. What was distinctive about the army and police was that they possessed the power to remove the source of the grievances which they shared with many civilians.

Like most civilians, the officers who led the coup had a clearer idea of what they were 'against' than what they were 'for'. There was little to suggest that the new Government felt that it had any mission to transform society, as Colonel Nasser apparently felt in Egypt. Indeed, as we shall see later, it stressed its faith in the chieftaincy, private enterprise and good relations with the West, and with Ghana's Francophone neighbours. Despite talk of a 'revolution' and the dawn of a 'new era', the policy pronouncements of the new rulers suggested that they wanted to restore much of the political landscape which had existed at the time of independence in 1957 and which they felt had been eroded by such measures as the Republican Constitution, which established an executive president, the creation of a one-party state, the increased presidential control over the chieftaincy and the 'socialistic' seven-year plan. Only three days after the coup, the new rulers proclaimed their anxiety to hand over power to a duly-constituted representative civilian government 'as soon as possible', and announced their intention to appoint a constitutional commission to prepare a constitution in which 'the sovereign power of the state would be fairly and judiciously shared between the executive, legislature and judiciary, and which would make the concentration of power in the hands of a single individual impossible'.[8] Two days later, the new head of Government, General Ankrah, made it clear that there were no plans for further nationalization, and that the structure of the existing state corporations would be reviewed.[9] These statements tempted observers to pin a variety of ideological and sociological labels on the military Government: 'Sandhurst trained' (only one member was), 'middle class' and 'pro-Western' were frequently used. If one tries to explain why Ghana's senior army and police officers held the values they did at the time of the coup, the explanation can be found partly in a pragmatism common to most Ghanaians, and partly in terms of the education and training they had received. Seven of the eight members of the military Government had attended mission schools, and all had received military or police training in Britain. They had thus been exposed to the sort of Western values which many of the civilian politicians they had ousted despised. In particular, the uniformed officers believed that many institutions, including their own, should be shielded from the direct control of politicians, and they felt threatened by the sort of monolithic state which Dr Nkrumah had been trying to build. The pragmatic approach to economics and foreign affairs would probably have been adopted if the Government had been formed by drawing out of a hat the names of any eight Ghanaians with secondary education. There were few who wanted to continue with Nkrumah's brand of socialism, or any other brand, and there was a broad consensus in favour of any policies which would reduce the everyday hardships caused by inflation and shortages; hence the attacks on 'prestige spending' and 'wasteful' public enterprise.

Seen in a broader context, the desire of Ghana's new rulers to return from the one-party state to the pluralistic politics of earlier years is in accordance with S. P. Huntington's generalizations about the difficult political attitudes of soldiers:

> In a world of oligarchy, the soldier is a radical. In a middle class world, he is a participant and an arbiter; as mass society looms on the horizon, he becomes a conservative guardian of the existing order.[10]

Ghana in 1966 did not possess an entrenched aristocracy which would have made the country ripe for takeover by a Nasser. Neither did it have urban workers sufficiently organized to provide a base for a Perón. The majority of people were rural dwellers, and many were self-employed. Chou En Lai's observation that Africa was 'ripe for revolution' proved as inaccurate in Ghana as in other African states. There were very few people who saw anything to be gained for themselves from a radical social upheaval, and still fewer who possessed the means to bring such an upheaval about. It was much easier for people to perceive the sort of gains which might be realized by operating the political system inherited at independence more efficiently, with less corruption, nepotism and extravagance, and without a party based on an alien ideology. This was the perception which many members of the chieftaincy and the middle class had of Ghanaian politics in 1966, and the army and police officers, who shared many of the aspirations of these groups, were able to initiate not a revolution, but a return to older and more familiar values.

In a sense, the dislike of economic extravagance, arbitrary rule and corruption may imply a belief in the converse policies of retrenchment and the establishment of democratic institutions which make the abuse of power more difficult, but these aims are so broad that they cannot be realized by soldiers and policemen alone. They require the skills of economists, administrators, lawyers and politicians, and they require the co-operation of a wider public. The ultimate destination was the distant harbour of democratic civilian rule. Once this harbour was reached, the officers who had taken the helm would be able to retire to the Ghanaian equivalents of Cheltenham or Tunbridge Wells. Until that day arrived, there were many hazards to be negotiated. The chapters which follow will examine these hazards and the Government's ability, or lack of ability, to overcome them.

II : Putting Down Roots (1)

The inability of military rulers to write a manifesto before taking power is paralleled by their inability to canvass for public support until the dawn when they capture the nation's broadcasting network. Unlike many civilian regimes, their roots in society do not grow gradually through a series of communications with various social and political institutions. They have to be put down quickly after power has been acquired. Whether the Government is to be an autocratic one, forcing its will on an unwilling public, or a more sensitive one, trying as far as possible to please the people, some means must be found of keeping in touch with the man in the bush. The most obvious problems are the establishment of 'legitimacy', preventing threats to the Government's survival by those it has supplanted or by new groups, deciding what sort of concessions can be made to different sections of the public, and what degree of personal freedom can be permitted. The word 'can' is used rather than 'should', since freedom, conciliation and repression are not commodities which governments can simply provide in varying quantities as the mood takes them. The proportion in which each is provided depends largely on the extent of inter-dependence between the Government and different sections of the community, and on the severity of threats, real or imaginary, to the Government's survival. These factors in turn depend largely on the structure of the society in which the Government is operating. This chapter will consider these factors in Ghana between 1966 and 1969. It will begin with the immediate problems of establishing legitimacy and preventing the return of the former rulers. It will then consider the social framework in which public opinion operates in Ghana, and the extent to which the change of Government in 1966 altered relations between Government and governed. The method of forestalling any new threats to those in power will be examined in Chapter III, as will the limits to personal freedom.

Establishing Legitimacy

'Legitimacy', in the political sense, is normally taken to mean public recognition of a ruler's right to rule. To acquire this recognition rulers may use a variety of justifications for occupying their positions, from success at the polls to divine right. In Ghana, the justification was that the army and police had used the only means available of removing a dictator, and were holding power only for as long as was necessary before arrangements could be made for free elections. Their defence was that only undemocratic methods could be used in pursuit of the ultimate goal of democracy.

According to Dr Nkrumah, who was in China at the time, demonstrations of support for the military Government only occurred after instructions from police headquarters, when unwilling demonstrators marched through the streets carrying banners prepared in advance in the American Embassy.[1] This is crediting the new rulers with a greater flair for public relations than they possessed. Not even the name and composition of the new Government were settled until after the shooting had ended. The name 'National Revolutionary Council' was suggested, but General Kotoka wanted to make it clear that the aim was to liberate the nation from Nkrumah, not to change the structure of society, and he persuaded his colleagues to adopt the title 'National Liberation Council' (NLC). It was originally proposed that the council should consist of four army and three police officers (five of whom had apparently had advance knowledge of the coup), and it was only five days after the coup that another police officer, Anthony Deku, was added.

Despite the NLC's inexperience in the field of public relations, there was little need for it to justify its assumption of power to most of the public. News of the coup was broadcast at dawn,

and people were dancing in the streets of Accra even before the
army had gained control of the former president's headquarters
at Flagstaff House. Congratulations reached the NLC from
chiefs, civil servants, farmers, the Ghana Legion and the Horse
Racing Commission within a week of the coup.[2] Demonstrations of support were held by the people of Sekondi-Takoradi,
Kumasi boxers, 5,000 people at Ho, the YWCA, ex-servicemen
and Accra teachers. The Accra Jockeys carried a placard proclaiming that 'Even Horses are Free Without Nkrumah'.[3]
Church services were held to give thanks for what had happened.[4]

The public were eager to shower gifts on the new rulers to the
extent that the NLC needed to state that all donations were
voluntary. Typical was the report that the Association of
Kwahu Citizens had presented the NLC with £1,200, a sheep,
corned beef, yams and twenty cases of sardines. Most of the
gifts went to the National Relief Fund for released detainees.
The presentation of gifts to new rulers can be explained partly
in terms of traditional custom, but in so far as there were any
motives of self-interest, the donations suggest either fear of the
new Government or a willingness to please it. As reports of
massive demonstrations of loyalty to the Government had been
equally common before the coup, sceptics might ask how far
such activities were 'stage managed'. If they were, it suggests
that the public were remarkably pliable. At worst, the new
Government had to deal with people who would support who-
ever provided their bread and butter; at best, it enjoyed the
goodwill of people disillusioned with the previous Government.
This remarkable shift of people's loyalties suggests that Ghana
belongs to the group of countries classified by S. E. Finer as
having a 'low political culture'.[5] The phrase is, of course, used
in a non-emotive sense, just as economists classify some
countries as 'underdeveloped'. In accordance with Professor
Finer's definition, the politically relevant public, that is, the
section of the public able to exert influence on the Government,
is relatively narrow, and opinion is less resistant to military

intervention than where the 'political culture' is more developed. To many Ghanaians, national government, if the
concept has any meaning to them, is not seen as the outcome
of a popular choice, but as something beyond their control,
like the weather. A coup might be celebrated in the way that
people celebrate the end of a drought. But there remained a
minority who spoke the language of modern politics, and an
outside world to which the NLC looked for the economic
assistance it needed, and this required a formal claim to
legitimacy.

The immediate justification given by the NLC for seizing
power by force was, as we saw in Chapter I, the need to remove
an arbitrary dictatorship which had destroyed individual
freedom and created economic chaos. This was the theme of the
NLC broadcast immediately after its seizure of power.[6] The
broadcast by General Ankrah on 1 March elaborated on the
theme that constitutional methods of changing the Government were not available, and he referred to the African tradi-
tion of deposing chiefs who exercised power arbitrarily.[7]

The justifications were sufficiently broad to attract the support that the NLC needed. Everyone can be against dictatorship, corruption and austerity, and there was no immediate
official hint that those behind the coup were furthering a
sectional interest. The new rulers quickly formalized their
assumption of power by suspending the 1960 Constitution and
proclaiming their right to rule by decree.[8] Promising, like most
military rulers, to stay in power only temporarily, the NLC
announced, within two days of the coup, their intention of
appointing a Constitutional Commission so that they could
hand over power to 'a representative civilian government' as
soon as possible.[9]

Preventing the Former Rulers' Return

The army and police chose to take power while President
Nkrumah was on a diplomatic visit to China. They reasoned

that, in the President's absence, the coup would involve a
minimum of bloodshed and a maximum chance of success, but
there was the disadvantage from the NLC's point of view that
Nkrumah was still at large to mobilize resistance after the
coup. He took up residence in Guinea, from where he made
regular broadcasts to the people of Ghana for several months
after the coup, but in exile, as in power, his bark was usually
stronger than his bite. The picture he gave of a reign of terror
under the NLC was so much at variance with his audience's
own experience that he did little to enhance his reputation.[10]
All his lieutenants within Ghana were arrested immediately
after the coup, and several of his ministers were eager to
denounce their former leader. Kofi Baako, once a leading
exponent of Nkrumaism, claimed that if someone could eaves-
drop at the prison, they would know 'our' attitude to Nkrumah,[11] Krobo Edusei condemned Nkrumah's corruption,[12] and
Kweku Boateng, the former Minister of Science, complained of
ministers having been reduced to gaping sycophants.[13] Kwesi
Amoako-Atta, the former Finance Minister, condemned
Nkrumah's insensitivity to people's hardships,[14] and Alex
Quaison-Sackey, the former Minister of External Affairs, made
a similar criticism after returning to Ghana from the entourage
Nkrumah had taken to Peking shortly before the coup.[15]

Short of armed attack from Guinea, there seemed no means
by which Nkrumah could return immediately. Against this
background, a discussion of resisting attempts to restore him
to power may seem irrelevant, yet the NLC felt the need to
're-educate' people who had been exposed to Nkrumaist
ideology. The broadcast which followed the coup announced
that 'the myth of Nkrumah' had been broken. After such
obvious steps as removing the ex-president's statue and re-
naming streets and institutions previously named after him, the
new Government had the task of emphasizing Nkrumah's
shortcomings and explaining Ghana's achievements in terms of
the work of the whole nation rather than one man, in order to
put the NLC's aims and policies in a favourable light in contrast

with its predecessors. The image presented of Nkrumah's Ghana was one that wasted resources on prestige projects and supported subversion in other parts of Africa, while living standards of the Ghanaian people deteriorated. These were the points emphasized by General Ankrah in his broadcast on 1 March 1966.

In the short term, the return of the Convention People's Party (CPP) did not appear to offer benefits to anyone beyond party members (most of whose leaders were in prison) and those benefiting from party patronage, many of whom might find it easier to seek other patrons than to try to change the Government. In the long run, the possibility of the former rulers returning to power might depend on how memories of their record compared with the performances of the new Government. Having banned the CPP and condemned its works, the NLC still felt it necessary to organize a campaign through the Ministry of Labour and Social Welfare to 'destroy the image of Nkrumah', a move they felt especially necessary in the rural areas.[16] Seven hundred towns and villages were to be visited in a campaign to explain the reasons for the coup. To meet more distant problems, a series of decrees were passed to disqualify many members of the former regime from holding political office after the return of civil rule.[17] Beyond this there seems to have been little attempt to replace one ideology with another. As commissions of inquiry were appointed into the various activities of the Nkrumah Government, and charges of its corruption and waste became more widespread,[18] the need for any formal 're-education' appeared to become less. By early 1968, many of the Ghanaians who had gone into exile in Guinea with Dr Nkrumah had returned and it was increasingly obvious that, in trying to prevent the restoration of the former regime, the NLC was using a sledgehammer to crack a nut. Even when party leaders were released from prison there was no longer any popular base on which they could build.

Public Opinion: The Ghanaian Setting

Certain features of society are important in influencing the relationship between government and governed, irrespective of who forms the Government at any particular moment. Ghana's total population is well under ten million and those with secondary education form only a very small proportion of the total, only 30,340 according to the 1960 Census.[19] While the total population is small, families are large. The personal contacts of a man in a high position may be broad because he has known others in similar positions since his schooldays. They may also be deep, because most relations will not have climbed the social scale with him. Given this sort of background, a series of informal contacts exist between government and governed, with the result that a person in authority may be lobbied as much by old school friends, former undergraduate colleagues or relatives with varied contacts, as by formal groups.

Such pressure groups as exist, as in most 'developing countries', often have little formal organization and may have little to contribute to political debate beyond shouting 'I want'. Ghana does, however, possess some important groups that do more than this. The Trades Union Congress has over 400,000 members, a large full-time staff and a headquarters as grand as any modern building in Accra. In addition to taking up demands for better wages and working conditions, it has contributed views on broader issues such as the cost of living.[20] The Ghana Chamber of Commerce also has a nationwide membership and had 500 affiliated firms in Accra alone. It has made a regular practice, even under the CPP, of sending memoranda to the Finance Minister before the preparation of the budget. Under the NLC both bodies were well represented on consultative committees, such as the Labour Advisory, Trade Advisory, Logistics and Ghanaian Enterprises Committees. A useful guide to Ghanaian pressure groups is provided by the decree of November 1968 which established the Constituent Assembly.[21] Ninety-one organizations were to be represented in the Assembly, from the regional Houses of Chiefs to the Ghana Midwives' Association and the National Catholic Secretariat.

A second important feature of Ghanaian society, in common with other societies at a similar level of development, is that of not 'standing up to authority'. This is not merely due to fear of preventive detention or protective custody. The eccentric who devotes his time to advocating policies that the Government is unlikely to adopt is a rare bird in Ghana. The Opposition boycotted the regional assemblies in 1957 instead of fighting a losing battle within them; many pressure group leaders gave up sending memoranda to the CPP Government once they believed that the Government had a closed mind. After the coup, it was the CPP members who remained silent, despite the opportunity to contribute their views to the Constitutional Commission, the Electoral Commission and numerous other investigatory and advisory bodies that helped to shape the political future.

The third feature, which distinguishes even the most autocratic African states from totalitarian countries, is the ability of people to 'vote with their feet'. Under Nkrumah this was the course followed by several senior civil servants who sought employment elsewhere when they found the regime intolerable. Other groups had the same potential power. Teachers who disliked party indoctrination in schools might quietly ignore instructions from above; cocoa farmers discontented with the low price of cocoa might grow something else instead. In 1969, importers reacted to the 5 per cent surcharge on imports by hoarding goods until the surcharge was reduced. Both before and after the coup, groups of ratepayers withheld their rates as a protest against the lack of public spending in their areas. (In other cases they have withheld them simply because they dislike parting with their money, and the machinery of local government was too weak to do anything about it.) As long as the Government is unable to coerce unco-operative individuals and groups (and sometimes unwilling to coerce them given the diversion of resources this would require), it may have to trim its policies to placate them.

Public Opinion Before the Coup

The CPP liked to regard itself as a monolithic body expressing the general will – 'The CPP is Ghana'. Sovereignty lay with the people. The people had chosen Nkrumaism. No one should obstruct those in authority from implementing the general will. Bing suggests that the CPP favoured building a party directly responsible to the masses, in contrast to the Opposition United Party, which had favoured a party meeting public opinion through traditional forms.[22] John Tettegah, the TUC's secretary-general, stressed the trade unions' role in explaining policy to the workers, with little mention of articulating the workers' demands. In his 79-page booklet on 'the role and task of trade unions', a chapter of only two pages is devoted to 'Ways of Raising the Living Standards of our Working People'.[23]

It is difficult to find any belief within the CPP that pressure groups or individuals had useful opinions or knowledge to contribute. Speeches by party leaders emphasized the need for loyalty to the party and president and for the study of party ideology. A speech on this theme by O. Owusu-Afriyie, Minister of Labour and Social Welfare, at an Eastern Region durbar was typical of thousands.[24] So were those by S. K. Tandoh, head of the Party Bureau Organization, asking district commissioners to work together with MPs to ensure absolute peace and the maintenance of party solidarity,[25] and E. M. Yakubu, the Nanton district commissioner, on the need for regular payment on basic rates and loyalty to the President.[26] Rallies held in June 1965 to introduce unopposed CPP candidates to their constituents helped to emphasize the leaders' view that political initiative should come from above. Even the totalitarian refinement of allowing the people to legitimize their rulers' authority by voting for unopposed candidates was not adopted.

J. M. Lee suggests that MPs were primarily expected to represent the Government in their constituencies.[27]

The importance of having a mass party containing representatives of all sections of the community was stressed. In a broadcast after the 1964 referendum to approve the creation of a one-party state, Dr Nkrumah spoke of Parliament's future as a corporate body 'made up of farmers, workers, artisans, factory workers, teachers, technicians, engineers, managers, intellectuals and university professors, doctors, members of the Civil Service, public boards and the Judiciary', but the whole tone of speeches by politicians at all levels was that the function of people within these groups was to co-operate in implementing Nkrumaist ideas. R. E. Dowse suggests that Nkrumaism maintained that inquiry had become redundant in the face of certainty; all that remained was exposition.[28]

All this is not to say that no freedom of expression existed, or that the demands of particular groups could always be ignored. After the coup, Nkrumah wrote nostalgically about 'vigorous and unrestricted debates in the National Assembly', and free and open discussion of policies throughout the country. He also mentioned attempts to accommodate the middle class and chiefs 'despite their non-socialist views',[29] indicating something short of the totalitarian model. Bing notes that considerable freedom of expression was possible in Parliament 'almost to the last'.[30] Plenty of examples can be found of MPs criticizing ministerial policy, and even of ministers criticizing each other, notably in October 1962, when the Minister of Agriculture criticized the Minister of the Interior on such a sensitive issue as the operation of the Preventive Detention Act.[31] Criticism of authority was never completely eliminated. In June 1965, S. I. Iddrissu MP demanded that a committee be set up to investigate the properties and accounts of people in high positions, including MPs and Ministers.[32] The *Daily Graphic* was able to quote the case of a friend of the Minister of Trade, A. Y. K. Djin, who was the only African able to get a licence to import biscuits, under the headline 'Djin is my Business

Friend'.[33] No attempt was made to suppress all criticism all the time, but the Government always had the weapon of preventive detention to silence those whose views it did not wish to hear. Patrick Quaidoo's dismissal from the Government and subsequent detention in 1961, following his criticism of the Nkrumah personality cult, showed one area of criticism that would not be tolerated, and no one publicly ventured into this area again while Nkrumah was in power, apart from the (British) Bishop of Accra, who was promptly deported. Other targets of criticism were less closely guarded, as the examples quoted above suggest, and attacks that steered clear of the President and the party's claim to political monopoly were permitted.

In turning from the expression of public opinion to its influence on policy, interviews with pressure-group leaders suggested a situation in which whom you knew was usually more important than whom you represented. Even those fortunate individuals who were in favour found it increasingly difficult to influence the Government from 1960 onwards, and found the Government's reactions increasingly unpredictable. Among the individuals said to have had influence were John Tettegah of the TUC and Martin Appiah-Danquah, secretary-general of the United Ghana Farmers' Co-operative Council. Both led bodies that were 'wings of the party', and, as prominent party comrades, they had access to the president, and were said by ministers to have brought benefits to their members in terms of loans to farmers, many of which were not repaid, and a greater overmanning of public corporations than economic conditions required. The anti-Nkrumaists complained that the Government frequently gave directives without consulting those affected,[34] while Nkrumaists tended to ignore the existence of pressure groups by assuming that the mass party alone decided priorities. In practice, the positions may have been more complicated. R. E. Dowse describes a political élite almost impregnable even to Nkrumah, containing 'a jigsaw puzzle of mutually reinforcing and protecting jobs, bribes, malpractices, nepotism and sexual partners'. Nkrumah, he claims, could never do more than threaten to bring the CPP to heel.[35]

This might suggest no more than an oligarchy, rather than a government sensitive to public opinion, but Bing suggests that there was at least one pressure group that could not be ignored. Describing Nkrumah's problems in 1961, he claims that the President was unable to make a popular appeal against the corrupt elements in the CPP, as he had already alienated the industrial side of the party through the budget.[36] At worst, autocracy was modified by the need to avoid upsetting all the people all the time, yet pressure groups possessed few sanctions apart from unconstitutional action, or the sort of 'voting with their feet' already described. Even the industrial workers failed to get the concessions they demanded in the most important strike of the post-independence period, that of September 1961, and many of the strike's leaders and alleged supporters were imprisoned. The leadership of the trade union movement, significantly, opposed the strike. Tettegah's attitude (quoted above) suggests that they were party men first and labour leaders second. As long as the CPP was able to absorb pressure-group leaders so that they depended more on the party than on those they nominally represented, the scope for groups influencing the Government was limited. Tettegah claimed after the coup that 'Nkrumah feared me – that is why I was forced to leave the Ghana Trades Union Congress to be replaced by his own nominees'.[37] A similar picture of initiative coming from above was given in the case of the farmers by Nkrumah's Finance Minister, Kwesi Amoako-Atta, two days before the coup. The United Ghana Farmers' Council had, he said, no complete register of members, and the power of officials tended to flow from Accra.[38] The Ghana Muslim Council appears to have been similarly dominated from above. Its executive members were dismissed in March 1966 on the grounds that they had been 'imposed' by Nkrumah.[39]

With wings of the CPP covering farmers, trade unions, women, students and youth, and with the Government controlling the appointment and dismissal of chiefs, the ability of pressure groups to articulate public opinion or to influence the Government would appear to have been extremely limited. Leaders could become isolated from rank-and-file through party patronage, and those who initiated demands from below, such as the 1961 strikers, could be imprisoned.

Groups not affiliated to the party, such as the churches, the chieftaincy and business, found it increasingly difficult to get a hearing. A vicious circle developed in which people became less and less willing to speak their minds, as they saw their fellow citizens put in detention for speaking theirs, with the result that ministers became unable to obtain the opinion of experts or 'interested parties' even when they genuinely wanted them. When an institution was not integrated into the ruling party, it might still be pressed into choosing party officials to lead it, so that even a nominally independent body, like the Ghana Association for the Advancement of Management, 'elected' politicians to its most important offices. The imprisonment of two managers who criticized government policy, not from a public platform but in company correspondence, showed how far repression could sometimes go. There were occasions when people made quite sweeping criticisms without any unfortunate results, but the unpredictability of the Government's reaction made it safer to keep quiet.

Public Opinion After the Coup

After February 1966, many groups that had for long kept their demands bottled up began lobbying the NLC, and in the freer conditions that now prevailed, new groups came into being. A random list of bodies reported in the press to have made demands on the Government includes the Ghana National Landlords and Tenants Association, the Ghana Teachers' Association, the Ghana Co-operative Distillers, the Ghana Chamber of Commerce, the Ashanti Football Pools Agents, the National League Clubs' Association, the Eastern Region

Transport Co-operative Union, the Ghana Boxing Authority, the Ghana Co-operative Farming and Marketing Association, the Western Region farmers, the Eastern Region farmers, the Kumasi Horse Owners' Association, the Brong-Ahafo Fish Marketing Co-operative Union, the Koforidua bread bakers, the Greater Accra Fishing Co-operative Union, the Tafo farmers, the Osco Shipping Company, the Ghana Manufacturers' Association, the Ghana National Farmers' Union, the Ghana National Contractors' Association, the Brong-Ahafo importers, the Ghana Private Road Transport Union, the Ghana Alcohol Distillers and Sellers, the Accra street hawkers, the Ghana Hoteliers and Caterers' Association, W. Biney and Company, the Ghana Bar Association, the Aborigines' Rights Protection Society, the nurse anaesthetists, the Accra bus workers, State Housing Corporation tenants at Ho, the Ghana Muslim Association and numerous trade unions.

Several factors made the relationship between the Government and pressure groups different after the coup. The most obvious ones were due to the new Government's different claims to legitimacy, its different ideology and its greater ignorance and inexperience at the time of assuming power. The NLC could not pretend to reflect a 'general will' by presiding over a mass party with 'integral wings', and it destroyed most of the nominally democratic machinery by suspending the Republican Constitution. This left only pressure groups as a means of contact with the public. Ideologically, the speeches made by NLC members contrasted with those of their predecessors. General Ankrah, speaking of the functions of regional committees of administration, mentioned the need for them to advise the Government on public reactions to its policies, and to inform it of the needs of the people.[40] Speaking at the University of Ghana, he asked the universities to take the initiative on matters of interest or concern to them and to send their 'well-considered advice' to the NLC.[41] General Afrifa asked Ghanaian intellectuals to be bold enough to criticize the NLC if they considered any of its actions wrong.[43] General

Kotoka asked for criticism 'that helps us to see alternative and better solutions'.[43] Of the NLC members it was only in the speeches of Inspector General Harlley that it was difficult to find references to the importance of public opinion. Harlley's speeches on the need to root out the subversive and corrupt, and to end illegal strikes, were more reminiscent of the Nkrumaist period. His warning that 'enemies of the revolution' who tried to disrupt the civilian rule programme would be 'dealt with'[44] was fairly typical of his tone. For the NLC as a whole, the lack of commitment to any rigid programme at the time of assuming power made it easier for it to listen to demands from below. The NLC lacked the experience, and possibly the desire, to govern without the aid of pressure groups. This inexperience, combined with the NLC's narrow occupational base (confined to soldiers and policemen) which made it more ignorant of the life of many sections of the community, increased its dependence on pressure groups. Its approach was frequently one of 'Take me to your leader'. This contrasts with the CPP slogan, printed at the top of one of its newspapers, 'The welfare of the people is the supreme law'. This carried the implication that a popularly elected government could ignore any group whose demands conflicted with the general welfare. The NLC, which could not claim a popular mandate, preferred to tread more warily.

Some of the NLC's critics claimed that public opinion was irrelevant in the determination of government policy. Bing claimed, over eighteen months after the coup, that the Government had so far been based on 'naked police and army rule'.[45] Nkrumah believed at about the same time that the NLC had suppressed 'any type of consultation with the people'.[46] It is difficult to accept these views when one examines the structure for consultation created by the NLC, though it is possible that the sections of the public most frequently consulted were those for which Nkrumah would have had little time.

A study of pressure-group politics in a country normally includes a classification of the groups that exist, a description of the points of contact that they have with decision-making authorities, and an attempt to assess the factors that determine the success of the Government or the groups in their dealings with one another. The most easily identifiable groups in Ghana cover education, traditional authority, public enterprise, co-operatives, private enterprise (both indigenous and foreign), the professions, labour, and religious and student bodies. Of these, the most important, in terms of interdependence with the Government during the NLC period, appear to have been traditional authorities and private enterprise. The former were needed to ensure support for and co-operation with the Government at the grass roots, while the latter were needed to implement an economic policy that relied more heavily on the private sector.

The party machinery for those points of contact that had existed under Nkrumah was swept away, but most of the formal Civil Service negotiating machinery remained intact, though the number of ministries was nearly halved. At the regional level, regional commissioners appointed from the ranks of MPs were replaced by regional committees of administration made up of soldiers, policemen and civil servants. At the local level, the number of administrative districts was reduced from 168 to 47,[47] with nominally elected councillors replaced by management committees, including originally a majority of central and local government officials,[48] but later a larger number of nominated politicians.[49] The main innovations by the NLC were the creation of a network of advisory committees and the appointment of numerous commissions and committees of inquiry, many of which contained representatives of pressure groups and so provided a means by which groups could convey their demands. Immediately after the coup the NLC appointed standing committees to cover administration, economics, external affairs and publicity. Committees on law, tenders, agriculture and logistics were added later.[50] A Political Committee was established in July 1966 'to make proposals to the NLC on modifications to enactments, decisions and policy to serve the public interest'.[51] An Expediting Committee was added in November 1966. The structure was altered in July 1967 when the Political Committee was replaced by a larger National Advisory Committee, and the Legal and Publicity Committees were dissolved.[52] While some of the committees were confined to civil servants and officers of the armed forces, others such as the Political, Legal, and Agricultural Committees, and later the National Advisory Committee, included 'outsiders'.

Some committees sought out pressure groups on their own initiative. The Agricultural Committee met farmers' representatives at all regional centres and discussed such matters as subsidies, the employment of more staff by the Ministry of Agriculture, roof loans and the release of forest reserve land.[55] The Economic Committee met representatives of the Ghana Chamber of Commerce, the Ghana Manufacturers' Association and the Ghana Employers' Association to discuss 'problems of common interest', shortly after its appointment.[56]

Commissions and committees of inquiry were set up to study a variety of problems inherited by the NLC on subjects as diverse as the operations of individual local authorities, Nkrumah's properties, the organization of individual academic institutions, the operation of several public corporations, the assets of CPP officials, the public services structure and salaries, TUC funds, import licensing, preventive detention, cocoa marketing, the educational system, the supply of school textbooks and sport. Commissions were also appointed to work out a new electoral system and to draft a new constitution. Apart from exposing the alleged sins of the previous regime, many of these bodies had power to make recommendations on future policy and were able to hear evidence from witnesses, many of whom were in practice the representatives of pressure groups. This was not an innovation introduced by the NLC, but the number of investigatory and advisory bodies was greater than under the previous regime, totalling over seventy in three and a half years. More radical changes could be recommended and accepted which, under Nkrumah, would have involved departures from socialist ideology, confessions of failure or dishonesty, and, in the case of loss-making corporations, a reduction in party patronage. Many committees and commissions included members who were 'interested parties'. Twenty-eight of the thirty-two members of the Educational Review Committee were employed in education;[55] three of the five members of the de Graft Johnson Committee on the Local Purchase of Cocoa were engaged in cocoa production or distribution.[56] On others, academics, lawyers, accountants, businessmen and civil servants were predominant. Six of the Constitutional Commission's original seventeen members were lawyers, and many critics of the Commission's report condemned the extensive powers it proposed for the judiciary.[57]

The description of the framework in which public opinion operated suggests differences between military rule in Ghana and elsewhere. Shils describes armies in new states as attempting to conduct a polity without politics and politicians, and of trying to run the country 'as if it were a large army camp', with consultative institutions suspended.[58] Pye, in the same volume, mentions how military rule in Burma ended open communication between ruler and ruled and destroyed any means of handling conflicting interests.[59] The different situation in Ghana can be attributed at least in part to the relationship between leaders of the army and police, and leaders of other institutions such as the bar, business, the churches and the chieftaincy, many of whom had provided the core of traditional and middle-class opposition to Nkrumah. All these institutions antedated the CPP, and many of their members preferred a political system in which they, as members of the 'élite', could negotiate directly with the Government, without the encumbrance of a mass party. Bing suggests that by 1964 the alliance between the CPP and the old African ruling class was broken, and 'that the way was now open for all those who had long been plotting against Nkrumah'.[60] Nkrumah, apart from blaming the 'imperialists' for the coup, saw links between

B

the old 'élite' and the army and police, and complained that the Civil Service and judiciary went over to the NLC 'almost to a man'.[61] General Afrifa expressed admiration for the former Opposition leaders, such as Dr Danquah and William Ofori-Atta, in his book justifying the coup.[62] This is not to accept journalistic myths about 'Sandhurst-trained officers' imbibing British values, though the education of seven of the NLC's original eight members at British mission schools and the training all of them received in England may have had an 'Anglicizing' influence.[63] What was of more immediate importance was that in rejecting the 'mass-party' politics of the CPP, the new rulers only had a limited range of practical alternatives to turn to. There was a preference for traditional rulers rather than the more self-made CPP rulers, and some admiration for the political values imparted by the British. Afrifa was 'ever prepared to fight alongside my friends in the United Kingdom'.[64] General Ankrah promised immediately after the coup to 'respect the institution of chieftaincy',[65] and later asked the chiefs to provide the necessary leadership to help revive the country's economy.[66]

Apart from the chieftaincy, the other major pillar on which opposition to Nkrumah had rested had been the 'middle class'. (This term is used in different ways by different people. In this study it can be taken to mean the minority of the population, which has received secondary education.) Many Ghanaian businessmen had opposed the CPP policies of taxing cocoa heavily and encouraging both public enterprise and foreign enterprise at the expense of local private enterprise, while many members of the professions had been disappointed that the political power they had expected had been snatched from them by the CPP when colonial rule ended. This is not to say that the cleavage in Ghanaian politics had been a simple one between a working-class CPP and a middle-class United Party, but the fact that a large middle-class element survived, which regarded CPP rule as against its interests, was important to those who seized power in February 1966. The fact that this group had certain class affinities with the army and police officers was an added reason for mutual co-operation between them.

The classification of African political parties into 'mass' and 'patron' parties may have its weaknesses,[67] but there is some value in distinguishing between those where a member's status in the party depends largely on his status in society, and those where his status in the party depends partly on the avenues of advancement provided by the party itself. In Ghana the United Party belonged to the first category, and the CPP to the second.[68] If the CPP policy of 'mobilizing the masses' had failed in the eyes of the NLC, the obvious alternative was to revert to the United Party policy of dealing with the public through pressure groups.

In discussing the determinants of these groups' successes or failures, the approach used below will be to examine a few of the demands of some of the stronger groups, to examine the Government's reaction and to consider what useful generalizations can be made on the basis of the information presented. The issues considered will be the restoration of some of the chiefs' power and influence, de-nationalization, the restriction of foreign enterprise and the restoration of spending on certain local projects.

The chiefs wasted no time in showing their attitude to the coup. The Asantehene, generally considered to be one of the most influential chiefs on account of his age and experience and the size of his chiefdom, welcomed the opportunity for chiefs to reign in peace now that Nkrumah had gone,[69] and the general reaction was that a usurper had got his just deserts. Demands were soon made for the restoration of various powers taken away by Nkrumah, and the granting of a few others, and for the restoration of chiefs 'improperly' deposed by Nkrumah. By January 1967 the Chieftaincy Secretariat reported that petitions over stool disputes were still 'pouring in'.[70] (The 'stool' is the chiefly equivalent of a royal throne.) The Omanhene of Akim Bosome demanded that paramount chiefs be

made district administrative heads.[71] Berekum Traditional
Council asked the NLC to restore stool land revenue to the
chiefs, and asked that petty disputes be settled in Chiefs' courts
instead of the ordinary law courts.[72] The Central Regional
House of Chiefs asked the NLC to repeal the 1962 Rents
(Stabilization) Act and the Rents (Cocoa Farms) Regulations
Act to provide revenue to 'enhance the prestige of the Chief-
taincy' and to benefit farmers and local people.[73] Akim
Abuakwa Traditional Council asked the NLC to repeal the
Stool Lands Amendment Act to enable traditional councils to
control lands and raise enough revenue to control traditional
areas.[74] The Northern Region chiefs demanded the transfer of
local courts' functions to traditional rulers.[75] The Omanhene of
Denkyira, in evidence to the Constitutional Commission,
suggested that chiefs should chair local councils.[76] The Eastern
Regional House of Chiefs asked the NLC to return land illegally
taken by the Nkrumah Government.[77] The Western Regional
House of Chiefs asked for the appointment of a commission on
chieftaincy affairs and for chiefs' salaries to be reviewed.[78]
Among the various demands for means of strengthening
traditional power in the new constitution, the demand for a
'no-party state' was especially great, with the apparent assumption that traditional institutions would be stronger if the
'modern' institution of parties could be banned.

The demands made by the chiefs suggest that they formed a
lobby skilled in making sectional demands appear to be in the
interests of the whole community, although they occasionally
spoilt their case by asking for more than they were likely to
get. (The demands listed above exclude those made for specific
favours for particular localities, which will be considered in
Chapter VI.) The NLC's most immediate concern appeared to
be to prevent the change of government from being used as a
pretext for settling old scores. General Kotoka attacked 'in-
discriminate destooling' and the wasting of money on litiga-
tion.[79] General Afrifa hoped that chiefs improperly appointed
by the CPP would voluntarily renounce their status to avoid

the complicated procedure of destoolment,[80] but by the end of May 1966 the NLC had directed the Chieftaincy Secretariat that chiefs destooled by Nkrumah for political reasons should report their cases to the clerks of the Houses of Chiefs. The Secretariat would then discuss the problems with the Houses of Chiefs and make recommendations to the NLC. By December, the Chieftaincy (Amendment) Decree had withdrawn recognition from 133 chiefs.[81] In August 1967 a further forty-three were destooled.[82]

In meeting demands for the removal of 'improperly' appointed chiefs it could be argued that the NLC was doing no more than meeting the wishes of the people in the various traditional areas. In listening to demands for increased power (or wealth) for chiefs, it had to balance their claims with those of other sections of the community, and to consider the consequences of meeting their demands within the context of national politics. Common courtesy aside, the chiefs' demands had to be listened to because the NLC wanted to secure their co-operation. The lack of even a nominal mass base meant that the only political platform the NLC and its appointees had in the rural areas was that provided by the traditional authorities. Even more than the CPP, the NLC's members had to rely on speaking at traditional 'durbars', with a local chief in the chair who would normally ask for various local amenities in the course of welcoming his guest. Typical of the sort of exchanges that took place were those occurring when Lt.-Col. Achampong, chairman of the Western Regional Committee of Administration, visited Mphor Traditional Area in December 1966. The Colonel appealed for more self-help projects: the local Omanhene appealed for pipe-borne water, a hospital and a police station in his area.[83] Beyond the need for a political platform, the speeches of NLC members and the officials appointed by them suggest the various ways in which they needed the chiefs' help. According to the secretary of the Western Regional Committee of Administration, they should ensure the regular payment of basic rates.[84] Commissioner of Police Nunoo spoke of their duty to maintain peace and stability.[85] The chairman of the Upper Regional Committee of Administration mentioned the need for chiefs' collaboration with district administrative officers to do the work previously done by district commissioners.[86] General Ankrah wanted chiefs to provide the necessary leadership in helping to revive the country's economy,[87] and to report all cases of hoarding.[88] None of these functions was completely new, but the loss of the co-operation of traditional authorities would probably have been more serious to the NLC than it would have been to the CPP, since the latter had alternative ways of enforcing its authority. Party officials and party organization, however rudimentary, had provided a possible means of by-passing chiefs that was no longer available. Apart from this, the NLC's policy of retrenchment, which caused considerable unemployment, made the loss of urban support a possibility, and to alienate the 'traditional' sector as well as the 'modern' might have made its position precarious.

The chiefs' demand for greater judicial power, which would have reduced the power of another strong group, the judiciary, did not meet with success, but many of the demands for a larger independent source of revenue were met in June 1966, when the 1962 Rents (Stabilization) Act was repealed 'to restore the customary rules of land tenure' under which the tenant farmer contributed a share of the proceeds of his crop to the owner.[89] In April 1969 it was decided that 40 per cent of stool land revenue should go to the chiefs, with the rest going to district councils.[90] The takeover of Ashanti Goldfields by Lonhro in late 1968 again demonstrated the ability of traditional authorities to enforce their claims to revenue from land. The Adansi chiefs petitioned the NLC, claiming that the takeover infringed their rights to the Obuasi gold mine.[91] At a meeting called to negotiate a settlement, the Commissioner for Lands and Mineral Resources admitted that the Government should have consulted the Adansi Traditional Council at the time of takeover.[92] The Council's success contrasts with the

more difficult task the Obuasi mine workers had in pursuing
their demands after the takeover, when they were only given
an (admittedly generous) goodwill award after disturbances in
which three miners were killed by the police.[93]

General Ankrah's broadcast shortly after the coup suggested
a preference for private rather than public enterprise. The NLC
had no plans for nationalization, but if nationalization were in
the best interests of the country, properly conducted negotia-
tions would be carried out. 'Structural changes' would be made
in the state corporations and some would be de-nationalized.
Active state participation would be limited to certain basic
and key projects, and healthy competition would be encouraged. Nkrumah's Seven Year Plan, which had given an
enlarged role to the public sector, was abandoned.[94] At this
stage there had been little time for pressure group influence,
and the General's statement was based mainly on the advice
of civil servants on the Economic Committee.

Most of the policies promised in Ankrah's broadcast were
subsequently carried out. In June 1966 the Ministry of Information listed seven state enterprises that were to be sold
and another eleven in which public participation would be
invited. Preferences could be given to Ghanaian entrepreneurs.[95] The structural changes outlined came with the
creation, in September 1967, of the Ghana Industrial Holding
Corporation, which took over nineteen state corporations.[96] It
was the method of carrying out de-nationalization, rather than
the policy itself, that gave rise to suggestions of pressure-
group influence. The *Daily Graphic* asked in May 1967 why
three of the few state enterprises to make a profit should be
among those to be de-nationalized, questioned the secrecy
over buyers' names [97] and criticized the decision to sell to the
highest bidders rather than to the existing managing directors.[98]

Channels of communication between Ghanaian private
enterprise and the Government were well provided for. Meetings of farmers and businessmen with the NLC's committees

shortly after the coup have already been mentioned. In February 1967, E. N. Omaboe, the chairman of the Economic Committee, promised the Ghana Manufacturers' Association that the tax system would be reviewed 'in view of their problems' and that joint consultative machinery would be set up between the Government and the Association.[99] In October 1967, the acting president of the Ghana Chamber of Commerce announced that agreement had been reached with the Government for loans to Ghanaian businessmen 'to overcome the insolvencies resulting from devaluation'.[100] In July 1968 the Commissioner for Labour and Social Welfare met a delegation from the Ghana Co-operative Distillers' Association to discuss methods of promoting indigenous business.[101] The 1967-8 Estimates for Agriculture mentioned the creation of an Agricultural Council to meet representatives of farmers and other interest groups 'to determine national agricultural policy'. The White Paper on the Promotion of Ghanaian Business Enterprises announced the creation of a committee that would include representatives of the Ghana Chamber of Commerce and selected Ghanaian businessmen to advise on the implementation of the plans outlined in the paper.[102] Some of the commissions and committees of inquiry enabled Ghanaian entrepreneurs to present their cases. The farmers were able to convince the Government, through the de Graft Johnson Committee, of the case for greater freedom for private and co-operative enterprises in cocoa buying.[103] The timber industry was similarly able to convince the Government through the Blay Commission of the need for tax and other reliefs.[104]

Apart from requesting favoured treatment for their own firms or industries, the main demands made by Ghanaian private enterprise were for lower taxation and greater protection against competition from foreign firms in Ghana. Budgets were generally favourable to local private enterprise. In August 1967 the property tax was abolished and the sales tax on local manufacturers was reduced.[105] The 1968 Budget reduced the taxation paid by Ghanaian companies, increased the taxation on imports with local substitutes and promised a review of bulk haulage rates (road haulage companies had withdrawn oil tankers from service in December 1967 due to 'lack of funds').

There was no mention in the early pronouncements of the NLC of restricting foreign competition in favour of Ghanaian private enterprise. This was an issue where pressure groups spoke first and the NLC acted afterwards. In September 1967 M. K. Batse, an Accra businessman, sent a memorandum to the NLC on the need to control Arab and Asian immigration, and to restrict the commercial activities of those already in Ghana. All the retail trade should, he said, be in the hands of Ghanaians.[106] Several letters to the *Daily Graphic* during the next three weeks expressed support for these views. At a meeting in Accra, W. A. Wiafe and Patrick Quaidoo, two businessmen who had been prominent in the CPP, added their weight to the view that the commercial activities of aliens should be restricted.[107] In December 1967, E. N. Omaboe, now the Economic Commissioner, announced the appointment of a committee to review immigration quotas with a view to curbing the influx of foreign nationals and encouraging the Ghanaian-ization of business. Questionnaires were sent to all firms employing expatriates, requiring information on their directors, the amount of capital they had in Ghana, details of expatriates employed and plans for training Ghanaians. A White Paper was published in 1968 announcing the restriction to Ghanaians, from 1 July 1968, of certain areas of business activity. These covered small-scale wholesaling and retailing; all taxi services; other small-scale businesses employing less than thirty workers or requiring 'unsophisticated techniques and/or fixed capital investment of less than 100,000 new cedis (N₵) (about £40,000) falling within the competence of Ghanaian entrepreneurs'; and the representation of overseas manufacturers, except where the Government gave specific permission to non-Ghanaians. Non-Ghanaians already operating in these areas were given time to transfer their business to Ghanaians.[108] A decree published in July 1968 prohibited the entry to and residence in certain parts of Ghana, mainly mining areas, by aliens.[109] The restrictions on foreign enterprise outlined in the 1968 White Paper were formalized by a decree published in January 1969. This decree empowered the Government to add to the list of restricted enterprises by executive instrument.[110]

The success of local groups in rescuing local projects from economy cuts was different from other pressure group activities so far mentioned, in that it involved not merely persuading the Government to take particular decisions but persuading it to change its mind. Among the projects which the NLC planned to cancel were the building of the Axim–Half Assini Road and the extension of Tamale Airport. It also proposed to close the Bibiani gold mine in the Western Region. The Axim–Half Assini Road was among the 'prestige projects' which the NLC announced its intention to cancel in June 1966.[111] General Ankrah, speaking at Tamale in August 1966, condemned the waste of £12 million on the airport when there was a need for dams, irrigation and feeder roads.[112] The decision on both projects was thus made after the NLC had been in power long enough to hear Civil Service advice, and could not be regarded as the mere reaction of naïve soldiers to what they regarded as the spendthrift policies of their predecessors.

Local opposition to the decision on the Axim–Half Assini Road was soon expressed. In August 1966 the Western Regional House of Chiefs appealed to the NLC to reconsider its decision.[113] The fact that the proposed road ran through Nzima territory, a group that had been well represented in Nkrumah's Government and was unrepresented on the NLC, and that it terminated in Nkrumah's home district, might have suggested that local demands would meet with little sympathy, but by the end of September, the Estimates approved for the Western Region included provision for resumption of work on the road.[114]

A hint of a change of policy over Tamale Airport came when G. Adlai-Mortty, the Special Commissioner for the Re-deployment of Labour, announced that the Government was reconsidering the resumption of work on the airport. 1,200 workers had, he said, been made redundant when the project was suspended.[115] In June 1967, Colonel Laryea, the chairman of the Northern Regional Committee of Administration, and the Northern Regional Chief Labour Officer, asked for the resumption of work as a means of reducing unemployment.[116] In April 1968, General Ankrah announced that a new international airport would be built at Tamale.[117]

Local pressure to save the Bibiani gold mine operated through both 'traditional' and 'modern' groups. In September 1967 the chiefs, the traditional council and the town development committee appealed for new industries to absorb the 2,000 workers who would be made redundant,[118] but the chairman of the Gold Mining Corporation announced that the workers would be transferred to other mines.[119] The local people then appealed through the Western Regional Committee of Administration for the reopening of the Bibiani North mine, abandoned during the war,[120] and Assifiri Danquah wrote an article in the *Daily Graphic* on the need for the Government to reconsider its decision on closure.[121] The Commissioner for Lands and Mineral Resources still insisted that operations at Bibiani would end within six months,[122] only for the Government to announce nearly a year later that a million new cedis (about £400,000), were to be granted for the development of new deposits at Bibiani.[123]

The NLC attitude suggested a willingness to placate the discontented or potentially discontented if this could be done without any radical changes of policy. Except in matters involving national security, there appeared to be a lack of 'toughness' in pursuing policies contrary to what one might expect from a military government. Instead of adopting the 'government must govern', 'right must prevail' approach, the emphasis was generally on taking a decision after listening to what all concerned had to say. One reason for this appears to have been the lack of a clear ideology, comparable even with the threadbare one of Nkrumaism. General Kotoka said that terms like socialism meant nothing to him.

> What people want is to be governed properly and honestly. They have their needs. Satisfy them; that is all.[124]

An approach like this had the advantage that issues were unlikely to be seen as 'matters of principle' and criticisms were less likely to be seen as heretical. Another possible reason for the 'conciliatory' approach may have been a fear of the channels into which discontent might flow in the absence of the ballot box, a popular base, or adequate means of coercion. An editorial in the *Legon Observer* suggested that most of the country's economic problems needed political solutions, but that the power structure of the NLC prevented it from imposing highly controversial political solutions, 'for the alternative to it [the NLC] would be anarchy'.[125]

In trying to reconcile pressure groups directly in conflict with one another, the NLC's attitude again appeared to be one of 'conciliation' rather than 'toughness', with a belief that conflicts could be resolved if only the 'proper channels' were used. Inspector-General Harlley told students to respect authority but insisted that the school authorities kept channels of communication with students open.[126] Commissioner of Police Deku, the NLC member responsible for education, also asked teachers to prevent student troubles by keeping the channels of communication open.[127] A similar faith in the use of proper channels was expressed in the field of labour relations, despite the fact that legal strikes were still virtually impossible throughout the NLC period.[128] After a miners' strike at Obuasi, General Afrifa spoke of the need for employers to give workers the opportunity to discuss their problems and to seek amicable solutions.[129] General Kotoka introduced new machinery for settling labour disputes in December 1966, involving the chairman of regional and district committees of administration, and regional and district labour officers, with appeals to the Ministry of Labour and the Trades Union Congress,[130] but

the number of strikes remained high throughout the period of
military rule. There were fifty-eight in the first two years,
thirty-eight in 1968 and fifty-one in 1969.[131]

General Ankrah returned to the theme of settlement by
negotiation in his 1968 New Year message,[132] though he
threatened illegal strikers with prosecution later in the year.[133]
Trade unions were among the most obviously discontented
groups throughout the NLC period. Almost as soon as General
Ankrah had resigned, the Secretary-General of the TUC
complained that the 'Ankrah administration' had 'stood behind
employers even in the light of naked injustice'.[134] Unions'
demands that the 1958 Industrial Relations Act be amended
to restore the legal right to strike were rejected, and union
funds were hit by the ending of compulsory membership, yet
even members of this section of the community expressed a
preference for the NLC over the previous Government, which
had denied unions any real independence.

There were occasions when the police were used to deal with
pressure groups that were felt to be getting out of hand and
were engaging in acts of violence against persons or property,
notably in the chieftaincy dispute at Yendi, the dispute between
rival Moslem factions at Kumasi, the strike at Obuasi gold
mine and a few student disturbances. On occasions the police
opened fire, but really 'tough' action was insisted on by the
Government only in cases allegedly involving national security.
Rail strikers who refused to return to work in September 1968,
after some of them had pulled up the track, were dismissed, as
were about a thousand employees of the Cargo Handling
Company after a strike in which it alleged that there were plans
for damaging installations at Tema harbour. Even in this case,
the 'toughness' was only relative. The strike leaders were not
put in gaol, as they had been in 1961, but were allowed to
appeal to the International Labour Organization, and the
workers were reinstated after the return of civilian rule.

In trying to secure a popular base, the NLC clearly did much
more than the minimum required to secure the people's co-

operation, but throughout its period in power it could never quite escape from the handicaps, or lose the advantages, that its method of capturing power had imposed. The major handicap was the fact that most of the channels of communication with the public were 'artificial' in the sense that specific machinery of consultation had to be created, or revived, in the absence of the sort of spontaneous contacts that usually develop when a country is run by civilian politicians, such as those in the CPP, who cannot break away completely from the groups that have helped them to win and retain power. A military government may appoint a committee to listen to the views of cocoa farmers; a civilian one may find it impossible to avoid listening to them, because of the contacts it has built up. Despite the apparent arrogance of the CPP there were times when it felt unable, or unwilling, to offend too many people. The failure to dismiss surplus workers in state corporations, quoted above, shows a 'softness' for which the NLC felt no need. This example suggests that the NLC's handicap could also be an advantage. If it was handicapped by not always knowing how the public would react to its policies, there were times when such ignorance enabled it to adopt the sort of measures from which civilian governments might have shied away. Consultation with the public was generally considered desirable, but it was not always as great a necessity as it might have been for a civilian government.

III · Putting Down Roots (2)

Threats to the NLC's Survival

Sources of opposition to the NLC might have come from within the armed forces, a re-formed CPP, a civilian pressure group, or a combination of these. Plots to overthrow the Government by all these types of group, except the CPP on its own, were proved or alleged at various times. Two former CPP members, one other civilian and an army lieutenant, were found guilty of conspiring to stage a counter-coup between November 1966 and January 1967.[1] Two army lieutenants were executed for attempting to stage a counter-coup in April 1967 in which they killed one NLC member, General Kotoka, and gained control of the nation's broadcasting network for a few hours.[2] In November 1968, Air Marshal Otu, the general officer commanding the Ghana Armed Forces, was arrested with his aide-de-camp, Lieutenant Kwapong, for complicity in subversive activity.[3] Inspector-General Harlley alleged their involvement in a plot to restore Nkrumah,[4] but the case was eventually dismissed and the officers were reinstated. On the civilian front, Harlley claimed that the Government had discovered a plot in 1967 involving strikes of railway and port workers aimed at the overthrow of the NLC.[5] Dr Nkrumah's claim that underground resistance to the NLC began immediately after the coup has already been noted.[6] In the face of these threats or alleged threats, NLC policy involved a mixture of coercion, patronage, administrative controls over the armed forces and policy decisions aimed at conciliating potential rebels.

The broadcast announcing the NLC's seizure of power required all senior CPP officials from constituency level upwards to report to the police, and the use of decrees placing individuals in protective custody made it possible to continue to imprison anyone without trial, including suspected subversionists. By December 1968 only twenty of those put in custody at the time of the coup remained there,[7] but the attempted counter-coup in April 1967 had led to the imprisonment of over 600 civilians and over 300 soldiers.[8] In January 1967 a decree was published allowing the use of military tribunals to try civilians suspected of attempting to overthrow the Government by force.[9] A decree published in October 1966 allowed the holding for twenty-eight days without a warrant, of any person taken into custody, subject to the Attorney-General's consent.[10] Political parties were made illegal from the beginning of military rule, though most of the NLC's members admitted that the ban was not always effectively enforced.[11] In so far as repressive laws can prevent a government's overthrow, the NLC was well protected.

While many leading CPP members were in gaol or exile, the NLC quickly brought former Opposition politicians into advisory committees and investigatory bodies. Ten of the seventeen members of the Constitutional Commission appointed in September 1966 had been members of opposition parties, as had thirteen of the twenty-three members appointed to the Political Committee in July 1966. Dr K. A. Busia, the former National Liberation Movement leader, was at various times after the coup, chairman of the NLC Political Committee, chairman of the Electoral Committee, chairman of the Board of the Centre for Civic Education, and chairman of the Committee on the Delimitation of the Functions of University Institutions. M. K. Apaloo, MP for Anlo South until his detention in 1958, was a member of the Political Committee, the Educational Review Committee, Ghana's representative at the United Nations, and a member of the Constitutional Commission. R. R. Amponsah, who had been general secretary of the National Liberation Movement in 1955 and had been detained in 1958, was appointed chairman of Ghana Airways in 1967, and served on the Political Committee, the Electoral

Commission, and the Ayeh Commission on the Erstwhile Publicity Secretariat. Even J. Kwesi Lamptey, who had lost his seat in Parliament in 1954 after leaving the CPP in 1952, and was described as a 'tutor at Fijai School' shortly after the coup, became chairman of the State Gold Mining Corporation as well as assistant headmaster at his school. With NLC patronage bringing much benefit to the former Opposition, threats to the state from this quarter appear to have been minimized.

Soldiers who have taken power from civilian governments by use of arms normally accept the possibility that other soldiers (and possibly policemen, sailors and airmen) may do the same to them, especially if they feel they are not getting their share of the spoils from the coup, and that the Government is now easy to topple. Lieutenant Arthur's justification for attempting a counter-coup in April 1967 included disappointment with arbitrary promotions of senior officers and the slow promotion of junior officers.[12] That Arthur came as near as he did to succeeding showed the vulnerability of the NLC. To try to make its position more secure, the Government arrested some of the senior army officers who were either suspected of involvement in the revolt or of 'sitting on the fence' until the outcome was clear. Eight senior officers lost their commissions and the officers commanding the army and navy were transferred to other posts. (These transfers were probably a punishment for failing to discover the plot. There is no evidence of these officers having actually been involved in it.) The police were instructed to report all troop movements. Most of the soldiers who chaired the regional committees of administration had their chairmanships made full-time, in the hope of preventing any individual from having too many contacts in both civil and military administration. The NLC decided to divest its members of many of their ministerial functions by appointing civilian commissioners to most ministries in June 1967, thus leaving more time for army and police duties. The combined effects of these arrangements, together with the steps the NLC took to show that its commitment to giving up power to civilians was genuine, prevented any further revolts in the army during the remaining two and a half years of military rule.

The 'conciliatory' attitude of the NLC in dealing with pressure groups has already been described. In trying to prevent strains on national unity, a similar attitude was adopted. While it has been suggested that members of the former opposition parties benefited from the coup, the coup did not mean a complete shift from CPP to United Party policies. The United Party itself had been formed in 1957 through the amalgamation of various opposition groups which had in common a dislike of the power wielded by the CPP. It included members of the National Liberation Movement, which had favoured federal government in order to give greater autonomy to Ashanti, while opposing the separation of Brong-Ahafo from Ashanti; members of the Togoland Congress, which had opposed the inclusion of the Volta Region within Ghana; and members of the Northern People's Party, which had favoured greater autonomy for the North. Despite the inclusion of so many former opposition politicians among its advisers, the NLC made few concessions to demands for regional autonomy and none to separation. Indeed, the inclusion of such people may have headed off many such demands, since there was now an opportunity for influence, and, with the return of civilian rule, power at the centre for politicians whose prospects had previously seldom extended beyond ruling individual regions. Despite its domination by former opposition members, the Constitutional Commission rejected any form of federalism. Dr Busia, once leader of the National Liberation Movement, insisted that the NLC would not force Brong-Ahafo to amalgamate with Ashanti,[13] and Inspector-General Harlley was quick to deny a newspaper report of plans to separate Ahafo from Brong.[14] All the regional boundaries drawn by the CPP thus remained intact.

One of the NLC's greatest problems in trying to maintain national unity was in deciding how to deal with former CPP members. Too much leniency might enable the CPP to re-form and challenge the Government's authority, although with hindsight, the lack of popular support for the former Government suggests that the prospect was remote. Too much repression or 'witch hunting' might have provoked resistance. The NLC itself appears to have been divided on how firm it should be. General Afrifa claimed in February 1967 that there was no need to be tougher, since an effective intelligence system existed,[15] but Kotoka spoke at the same time of the need for tough action when 'the CPP are re-grouping and alarming the countryside with threats of Nkrumah's return'.[16] Certain views appeared common to all those who had disliked the CPP. Its nominees should be removed from posts where their appointments were obviously 'political', inquiries should be conducted to establish how CPP leaders had acquired their assets, and very few of their members should serve on NLC committees, investigatory bodies or institutions that played any major part in policy formulation, unless they had clearly opposed the CPP from within. No one advocated the removal of CPP men from all positions of authority, if only because the party's large nominal membership would have made this an enormous task and their replacement impossible, and the NLC declared its opposition to any 'witch hunt'. The announcement of the release of 150 people from protective custody in April 1967 stated that this was done to help unify the country, to avoid the persecution and victimization of Nkrumah's followers and to aid national reconstruction.[17] Actions that reflected a broad anti-Nkrumah consensus included the freezing of the assets of members of the former Government and Parliament, and the appointment of three commissions of inquiry to investigate the assets of CPP officials.[18] General Afrifa admitted that failure to appoint these commissions earlier had led to the need for other measures to combat subversion, including the creation of military tribunals to try civilians.[19]

The question of the extent to which CPP men should be disqualified from holding public office under future civilian governments will be discussed in detail in Chapter VII. As far as the NLC period was concerned, none was appointed to any executive position and only four were appointed to advisory positions. Of those in Parliament on the eve of the coup, Mumuni Bawumia, the Minister of Local Government, and Jato Kaleo, an Opposition MP who had only joined the CPP when Ghana became a *de jure* one-party state in 1964, were appointed to the Electoral Commission, B. A. Bentum, the Minister of Forests, was appointed to the Political and National Advisory Committees, and J. A. Braimah, an outspoken backbencher, was appointed to the Political Committee. The other members of the former regime remained 'political outcasts'. If the CPP were to recapture power, they were clearly not going to be allowed to do so by penetrating the Government from within.

Limits to Freedom of Expression

Public statements by NLC members on their willingness to listen to pressure groups have already been quoted. On the expression of views through mass media, an equally tolerant attitude was expressed. Harlley assured the press of 'absolute freedom' and told Ghanaian journalists that they would not be restricted in their work, though he complained at one time of a general campaign against the police service in the press.[20] General Afrifa asked the press to offer more constructive criticism of the NLC and not to 'sing his master's voice'.[21] He wrote to one daily paper complaining that its attitude to the NLC was hardly different from that to Nkrumah before the coup and asked that, in the absence of an Opposition, the press should warn the NLC when it was going wrong,[22] but he had earlier distinguished between 'freedom of the press' and 'harmful, biased, destructive criticism'.[23] General Ankrah, too, suggested limits to freedom. The press was free to express any political opinion 'providing they do it constructively and responsibly'.[24] He complained in May 1967 of the press giving too much attention to the Middle East crisis and to 'trivial events' when the 'many positive strides of the NLC should command attention',[25] but the *Daily Graphic* asserted its independence by making events in Nigeria its 'lead story' in three of the subsequent four editions.[26]

The two main daily papers, and one Sunday paper, remained state-owned despite demands in their editorials for de-nationalization.[27] Commissioner of Police Deku argued that continued state ownership was necessary for the NLC in the absence of any other political platform,[28] but in practice considerably greater criticism of the Government occurred than under Nkrumah. Between 1960 and 1966 criticisms of individual ministers had been made, but never criticism of the president or Government as a whole. Within three months of the coup, the *Daily Graphic* felt free to print a letter attacking Ankrah's attitude to atheism,[29] and the same paper shortly afterwards contained a letter criticizing the NLC's practice of sending frequent congratulatory messages to foreign governments.[30] A letter criticizing the proposed Golden Triangle road network linking Ghana's three principal cities[31] showed again that allegations of 'prestige spending' were permitted. Possibly the most outspoken paper was the *Legon Observer*, run by a group of academics at the University of Ghana. One of its earliest editions criticized the practice of clearing roads of all traffic to enable the Head of State to pass;[32] a letter in a later edition asked if it was not fair 'to say at least something good of Kwame Nkrumah',[33] and the paper published editorials criticizing the Rumours Decree, which prohibited the publication of items which caused fear, alarm or despondency, disturbed public peace or caused disaffection against the NLC, and the 28-Day Custody Decree.[34] No restriction was placed on the importation of books critical of the NLC, and both Bing's *Reap the Whirlwind* and Nkrumah's *Dark Days in Ghana* were readily available,[35] but no one living in Ghana felt it prudent to write anything as critical as these authors.

On the negative side, many restrictions on freedom of expression remained. Political parties were made illegal immediately after the coup,[36] and people were prosecuted for forming parties at Nsawam, Mankranso and in the Western Region.[37] The ban was not lifted until five months before the end of military rule. The state continued to own two of the three main daily papers. Protective custody, like preventive detention before it, remained the ultimate weapon for dealing with those whose words or actions the Government disliked. In attempting to define the limits to freedom of expression, one can examine the statements made by those in power, the action taken against those who exceeded the limits and the types of opinion that did not appear in mass media.

Dislike by the NLC of 'harmful', 'destructive', and 'negative' criticism has already been mentioned, and some of its members spelt out what this meant in more detail. Commissioner Deku suggested that some press comments might be harmful, such as over-playing corruption in the police and thus helping Nkrumah to discredit the NLC.[38] General Kotoka spoke of the NLC's resentment of criticism that made its work difficult, and of the need to understand policy before criticizing it.[39] Remarks such as these may themselves have served as a warning to the press, especially in the state sector where, as Ankrah remarked: 'The one who pays the piper will have to call the tune.'[40] Direct use of the law against journalists and writers was rare. Rans Vigah of the *Evening News* was charged with breaking the Rumours Decree by reporting a theft of arms,[41] and Atta Mensah was gaoled for three years for writing 'defamatory' literature condemning the NLC.[42] However, other forms of pressure were used more frequently. The *Legon Observer* suggested that the dismissal of the editor of the independent *Pioneer* might have been due to pressure from 'a certain corporation of which he was critical and which threatened to withdraw its advertisements'.[43] Editorial dismissals that attracted more attention were those that followed criticism of the Abbott Agreement in 1967, which involved investment by an American firm in the State Pharmaceutical Corporation on terms regarded as highly favourable to the former. The NLC showed considerable tolerance in allowing the agreement to be debated on television in November 1967,[44] but when press criticism continued and raised the possibility of the American firm abrogating the agreement (which it eventually did), four editors were dismissed, without the civilian Commissioner for Information being consulted.[45] The line had apparently been crossed between constructive criticism, or even criticism that hurt the Government's pride, and criticism that weakened the Government's negotiating position. Many governments might want to silence their journalists in such a situation. The Ghana Government had the power to do so, and the temptation to use that power could not be resisted.

Opinions that hardly appeared at all in print included those that advocated the return of Nkrumah or the CPP, those suggesting the use of undue violence in the coup, and those that questioned the NLC's legitimacy or suggested corruption in the NLC. Asked what would happen if someone wrote to his paper praising Nkrumah, one journalist replied: 'Nobody knows what would happen. That's why they don't do it.' Unsure how far they could go, most people with unorthodox views played for safety. It is true that Nkrumah's and Bing's books were permitted, but both authors were a safe distance from Ghana. The minimum requirement of a writer within Ghana appeared to be to accept that, at worst, the coup did no harm. A. K. Armah's novel, *The Beautyful Ones Are Not Yet Born*, suggested that the coup merely replaced one group of exploiters with another, but even he showed no liking for Nkrumah. His hero, on being told that the army and police had seized power, remarked: 'I thought they always had power. Together with Nkrumah and his fat men.'[46]

Despite all these limitations, the contrast between the pre- and post-coup periods is real enough. Mass media were no longer regarded as tools for helping to build a Socialist state, required not merely to refrain from attacking the Government but to heap praise on it. There was no longer the assumption that those who did not shout loudly that they were with the

Government were against it. As long as he could avoid certain 'forbidden areas', the writer had considerable freedom of expression.

Why was Individual Freedom Enlarged?

We are left with the paradox that a government of men trained at Sandhurst, the Metropolitan Police Training College and similar institutions permitted greater freedom, both in the sense of allowing people to express their views in print and in the sense of encouraging consultation with the public in policy making, than the previous Government of civilian politicians who had proclaimed their faith in the liberation of all Africa. The difference can be explained partly in terms of personal inclination. Nkrumaism had been treated increasingly as a revealed truth which mere mortals had no right to criticize, whereas the NLC went out of its way to ask the people for their views, but the NCL's behaviour was influenced by the greater feeling of security which the NLC possessed. If the CPP Government had been oppressive, the oppression was not based mainly on armed force. More important was the network of contacts in which co-operation brought rewards and non co-operation brought the denial of rewards or preventive detention. This network of contacts required more subtle manipulation than the use of force, or threatened use of force, which the NLC was later able to use. Only by keeping a tight grip on the party and state machinery were those in power able to retain their positions. If they lost this grip, they would have depended more on the army and police as means of coercion, and it was not certain that their co-operation would have been forthcoming. Nkrumah admits in *Dark Days in Ghana*[47] that his relations with the police were not good, and it seems that he had long mistrusted them.

The NLC had three major weapons which enabled it to 'wield the big stick' if it felt that the greater freedom it had given the people was being misused. Firstly, it could use extra-

judicial powers in taking 'spectacular' decisions to impress
the public, such as the holding of a public execution after the
attempted counter-coup, and the use of soldiers to secure the
release of hoarded goods. Secondly, it was able to rule by decree.
Nkrumah had always felt the need to observe various constitutional refinements, including the use of elections and
referenda, albeit rigged, and the use of Parliamentary legislation. He usually achieved the results he wanted, but his
Government had to go through the motions of explaining,
justifying and meeting criticism. Even the amendment of the
Preventive Detention Act in 1963 was only achieved after
eight MPs had spoken against the Government. The NLC, by
contrast, could change the law by passing a decree without the
need for any public debate. It was thus able to take considerable power into its own hands through measures such as the
Rumours Decree, the 28-Day Custody Decree and the creation
of military tribunals for trying civilians. Thirdly, the NLC had
a virtual monopoly of arms. Naked force, or threats of it,
could always be used if all other methods failed, as was the
case in ending a violent chieftaincy dispute at Yendi, in securing the release of hoarded goods or suppressing strikes. This is
not to say that the NLC could have resisted a popular uprising,
but it had ample power to put down the sort of local disputes
between rival factions that sometimes occurred. Armed force
was made more effective by the intelligence systems which the
army and police controlled. Previously, Nkrumah had had his
own intelligence system, largely independent of the army and
police. The fact that they were able to overthrow him, and that
John Harlley, his own appointee at the head of the police,
played a major part in this, is a measure of the ineffectiveness
of that system.

Conclusion

Within a few months of taking power, the NLC had put down
roots in Ghanaian society which appeared to be deep enough to

enable the Government to withstand almost any political crisis that might come its way. If the arrangements for dealing with any internal army revolt appeared remarkably slack, until such a revolt nearly succeeded in April 1967, the measures adopted for securing civilian co-operation were remarkably successful. Having made itself popular by the mere act of overthrowing the CPP, the military Government capitalized on its popularity by taking steps to win favour with the groups on whom its success was largely dependent, including the chiefs, businessmen and academics, many of whom had once been Opposition politicians. Chiefs enjoyed greater power and prestige as a result of the change of government, private entrepreneurs were given greater scope, and academics benefited from the increased freedom of expression. These gains, together with the patronage bestowed by the NLC, helped to ensure that the NLC received the co-operation of the most influential sections of the community.

In terms of ability to stay in power, the NLC appeared to have many advantages. It was able to win public goodwill, initially by the mere act of overthrowing Nkrumah and later by taking measures to please various sections of the community, yet if there were any discontented elements that wanted to remove the Government, there were ample means of dealing with them. The basic need for survival was thus met, but governments do not exist merely to survive, they exist to carry out the policies they favour. It is to the problems encountered in executing these policies that we now turn.

IV · The Civil Service

With most members of the former Government in prison, and
many former Opposition politicians out of touch with day-to-
day politics, following long spells in prison or in exile, the only
obvious agency immediately available for implementing the
NLC's policies was the Civil Service. In attempting to assess the
role of the service during the period of military rule, this
chapter will consider the main policy aims of the NLC and its
perception of what part civil servants should play in achieving
these; the attitude of officials to their new masters' policies,
their capacity for doing the job they had been given, and the
sort of relationship between military men and officials that
emerged.

The NLC's Objectives

The largely 'negative' aims of the NLC have already been
noted. It had taken power because, it claimed, Nkrumah's
Government had created economic chaos, suppressed individual
freedom and helped the spread of corruption. There were a
number of spectacular, but uncomplicated, measures that could
be taken to place the new Government in a favourable light
in comparison with its predecessor. Over 800 of those who had
been imprisoned without trial were released, the frontiers with
Ghana's three neighbours were reopened, and stores of hoarded
goods were released by soldiers and policemen, who then sold
them at controlled prices. Plans were announced for the ending
of several 'prestige projects', corruption was to be rooted out
by the appointment of commissions and committees of inquiry
into the activities of various public bodies and individuals,
and a Constitutional Commission was appointed to prepare a

new constitution. The ultimate aim was to hand over power to a democratically elected civilian government, but the Ghana delegate at the United Nations announced two months after the coup that there would be no elections for three years, and most subsequent official statements suggested that military rule would not end before 1969. Having tried to impress public opinion at home and abroad with the actions described above, the question remained as to what the NLC was to do with the power it expected to wield for the next three years. Economic retrenchment, the re-negotiation of foreign debts, the restoration of the status of the chieftaincy, increased spending on the army to repair the neglect it had allegedly suffered; greater attention to the needs of Ghanaian private enterprise and a greater allocation of resources to rural development, were the policies most frequently emphasized.

The Administrators' Task

Very few civil servants had been let into the secret plans of the army and police officers who were to topple Dr Nkrumah, but the unpopularity of the Nkrumah Government as a result of economic hardship and what was felt to be a loss of personal freedom, and the ease with which the army had taken power in Nigeria a few weeks previously, meant that the coup of February 1966 was not unexpected, and the transition from a civilian government to a military one was remarkably smooth. The coup did not have any great effect on the internal organization of the Civil Service. The disillusionment of many officials with the previous Government, which will be discussed later, led to a greater willingness to co-operate with the new one, and this reduced the risk of its floundering as a result of sabotage or non co-operation.

The minimum arrangements necessary to prevent the country from being plunged into disorder were soon made. Secretaries to the former regional commissioners (all of whom had been politicians) were put in charge of the administration of the various regions, and the most senior civil servant in each district was put in charge of its administration.[1] It was not until nearly a month after the coup that regional administration was transferred to Regional Committees of Administration headed by army and police officers.[2] A decree passed in March 1966 transferred the functions previously performed by ministers to principal secretaries or heads of ministries, subject to the direction of the NLC,[3] and this remained the position until NLC members were given portfolios in June 1966. To assist in the formulation of new policies in place of the old ones against which the coup had been directed, four advisory committees were set up immediately, on economics, administration, publicity, and external affairs. Of the twenty-nine members of these committees, twenty-six were civil servants.[4]

The burden on civil servants was thus a heavy one. For nearly four months, senior officials were performing ministerial functions, and even the allocation of portfolios to NLC members did not reduce the burden appreciably. Eight uniformed officers, seven of whom still had full-time appointments in the army and police, could not easily control eighteen ministries between them, and much of the work normally performed by ministers was, in practice, left in Civil Service hands. This work included not merely working out policy within each ministry, but much of the work of co-ordination previously carried out through Cabinet Committees. No one suggested that these arrangements were ideal, but there appeared to be an expectation on the part of some NLC members that the delegation of work to officials would achieve better results than was in fact the case. A year after the coup, Inspector-General Harlley mentioned that committees had been reorganized several times in an effort to overcome the slowness of civil administration. General Afrifa spoke of the need for smaller committees to streamline administration, and General Kotoka deplored the lack of a sense of urgency. Due to his position in the armed forces he left most of his ministerial duties to his principal secretary but, he complained, 'things don't go as expected'. Commissioner of Police Deku shared with Kotoka a belief that the administrative machine could or should run smoothly, even when a minister headed several departments in addition to his military or police duties. He claimed that he was able to handle his substantive duties and the ministries under his control because he only dealt with 'policy matters'. Kotoka, at the time of his complaint, was in charge of Defence, Health, and Labour and Social Welfare, as well as being General Officer Commanding the Armed Forces. General Ocran was another NLC member who criticized the slowness in implementing policies. He complained that in his ministries, unlike the army, the line of authority was ill-defined and diffuse, and civil servants often did not know who was responsible for what.[5]

These remarks reveal as much about the men in power as they do about their officials. In interviews, civil servants pointed out that their masters failed to understand how much more complex the business of government was compared with the administration of a barracks. The vagueness of many NLC aims would itself help to explain why its members complained of Civil Service slowness in delivering the goods. They had not specified sufficiently clearly which goods they wanted, and officials had had to spend much time in deciding which appeared to be the most suitable.[6] Even when the aims were clear, the difficulties in achieving them were not always understood. One civil servant had had to point out to the officer in charge of his ministry that, just as one took trouble in setting up a gun correctly before firing it, so officials needed to ensure the same, or greater, attention to detail before embarking on a new policy. The analogy is obviously an imperfect one, and other civil servants suggested a failure by the Government to realize that, unlike firing a gun, policy decisions often involve choices between imperfect alternatives with compromises and adjustments, and consultation with the parties affected. Thus a change in the price of cocoa could not be made without taking into account the views of the State Cocoa Marketing

Board, the farmers, and the banks, and considering the effects on the economy as a whole. While the NLC was always eager to express its desire for individuals and pressure groups to have their say, and was frequently influenced by public opinion, there was at times a failure to realize that compromises on some issues would have repercussions on others.

How Adequate was the Civil Service?

The NLC and Civil Service were both handicapped by having to perform roles to which they were unaccustomed and for which they did not necessarily have the best qualifications. Before the appointment of civilian commissioners in June 1967, both had to help fill the vacuum left by the deposed politicians, in addition to carrying out their normal duties. The statements by Deku and Kotoka suggest that the greater part of the burden was borne by the Civil Service. NLC members inevitably kept certain areas of policy, such as defence and internal security, under close scrutiny, and they had to act as mouthpieces for their ministries in making policy statements, but most of the actual policy-making was carried out by officials, often through the newly-created committees, and only rarely did the Government make radical modifications to their recommendations.

To assess the adequacy of the Civil Service for the new tasks it had been given, we need to examine the state of the service at the time when the NLC took over. The ideal Civil Service, from the NLC's point of view, would probably have been one which, apart from possessing the obviously desired qualifications in terms of administrative and technical expertise, was capable of taking considerable initiative in offering advice on policy. It would have been willing to make strong criticisms if it felt its inexperienced masters did not understand the implications of what they were doing, but unwilling to become involved in policy making to the extent that the members became transformed into politicians. The Service's experiences under the

CPP Government did not provide an ideal training for the new role. Many of the ablest and most outspoken administrators, such as A. L. Adu, Robert Gardiner and J. H. Mensah, had left the country by 1966, disillusioned with the policies being followed and the way in which they were being carried out. For those who remained, criticism was never completely stifled, but officials complained that, as Nkrumah's 'socialist' and 'pan-African' policies became increasingly grandiose, so the area grew in which little notice was taken of criticism. If constructing a £10 million conference building or running a regular service of practically empty aircraft to the other side of the continent furthered these aims, then any official who questioned their wisdom was wasting his time, and possibly reducing his prospects of promotion.

Politics during the CPP period did not, however, consist entirely of decisions on spectacular pieces of investment. A whole variety of matters remained, once the general lines of policy had been settled, on which politicians were willing to be guided by the expertise of civil servants. Geoffrey Bing, who was in the Service throughout the period, modestly recalls that the Civil Service was confined within narrow limits, while the country was ruled by Nkrumah, his Cabinet, and various party and quasi-party organizations.[7] But it seems that some officials were confined within wider limits than others. From about 1960 onwards Dr Nkrumah felt less dependent on his party colleagues and, after attempts on his life, he felt increasingly suspicious of them, and turned for assistance to men with no political ambitions. Professor Austin noted that by mid 1963 'the ideological wing of the party was relatively subdued. . . . Nkrumah now placed his immense power behind his administrators'.[8] Some officials were undoubtedly allowed considerable scope in advising on policy, but the Service as a whole was handicapped serving under a government which insisted on willing the end even if there was no prospect of willing the means. Bing's observation that Ghana's purchase of VC10 aircraft was justifiable and that all that was lacking was the 'diplomatic negotiation of landing rights, the scientific prospecting of new routes and technical planning generally',[9] reflects what might either be regarded as a happy-go-lucky attitude towards the spending of other people's money or the pioneering spirit necessary to bring a backward country into the twentieth century, but it was not the sort of attitude that left much room for the traditional Civil Service function of advising on the practicability of policies.

The way in which civil servants had been brushed aside by the CPP had its effect when power was taken by a military government which expected to be 'pushed from behind' rather than 'held back'. The remarks of Deku and Kotoka, quoted above, suggested that if they did not quite expect their senior officials to produce rabbits out of hats, they did expect the sort of Civil Service initiative which the political environment of the previous six years had done little to encourage. Even where the principal secretary possessed the desired qualities, the patience of NLC members was often tried by inefficiency at lower levels, where simple clerical errors sometimes meant that there were unnecessarily long delays in providing villagers with pure drinking water or roads for marketing their crops, or even in calling routine committee meetings. This problem has been common to all Ghanaian Governments since independence, although its critics complain that the CPP made matters worse by a policy of patronage which took insufficient account of ability. For busy uniformed officers with no political experience, trying to prod officials at lower level, was one additional burden. General Ankrah, in his 1968 New Year broadcast, stressed the slipshodness, laziness, apathy, improper practices, lack of integrity, and ineptitude among public servants revealed by the Expediting Committee.[10]

In June 1966, three NLC members, Afrifa, Kotoka and Commissioner of Police Yakubu, all spoke within a few days of each other of the need for greater discipline in the Civil Service.[11] Kotoka complained that, in most cases, civil servants

c

had not re-dedicated themselves to the service of the nation
'since the revolution'. He claimed that, being used to military
discipline, the NLC had gone to the other extreme in trying to
suit civilians. It did not want to replace one form of suppression with another after the fall of Nkrumah, but it regarded
discipline as 'the foundation of efficiency'. He would make sur-
prise visits to his departments to check unpunctuality and
laziness.[12] Ankrah also concerned himself with the question of
punctuality. He ordered soldiers to lock out civil servants
arriving late at Osu Castle and warned the offenders of the
possibility of disciplinary action in the future,[13] an example
apparently copied from Nigeria. All this may have aroused
cheers from those who blamed bureaucrats for a variety of
national problems, but it is doubtful whether it made any great
difference to the extent to which the NLC's will was frustrated
by administrative inefficiency. Even when civilian commissioners took many duties from the NLC, interviews revealed
that they had to fight the same uphill battle.

Impatience of governments with their civil servants is not,
of course, something peculiar to Ghana. The nature of state
bureaucracies in many parts of the world is such that they are
unable to move at a pace which suits all politicians. In Ghana,
however, the bureaucratic routine, based on hierarchy and 'red
tape', was only part of the problem. The failure of some individual officials to follow any sort of routine made matters worse.

In terms of 'political neutrality', the Civil Service possessed
an asset that was invaluable to the military Government,
even if its importance was not fully appreciated in the beginning.
Most of Dr Nkrumah's efforts to give the Service a sense of
commitment to his policies and ideology were a failure. He
complained ruefully after the coup that 'the old civil service
and the Judiciary went over almost to a man to the usurping
regime'.[14] The loyalties of the Service were clearly to the state,
and not to any individual government or party. Under the NLC,
officials made every effort to maintain their 'neutrality'. It
was on the recommendation of the Administrative Committee,

manned entirely by senior civil servants, that responsibility for ministries was transferred from officials to NLC members in June 1966. While senior civil servants elsewhere were called on to attend Cabinet meetings of military Governments, and appeared to acquire an almost 'ministerial' status, their Ghanaian counterparts generally avoided 'political contamination'. As a result, the country was able to pass through the stages of the civilian Government of Nkrumah, a year of 'direct military rule', two years of government by uniformed men plus civilian commissioners, to the civilian Government of the Second Republic, with remarkable smoothness, without officials being involved in political manoeuvring. Commanding a Civil Service whose members, for the most part, had no political ambitions, the NLC was able to listen to advice in the knowledge that it was not offered for obviously selfish reasons.

The View from the Ministries

Ghanaian civil servants are no more homogeneous in outlook than civil servants in any other part of the world, but there were some views of both the CPP and NLC periods that were common to most of them. Some were sympathetic to the CPP's pan-Africanist and socialist aims while others wanted the state to do little more than provide the infrastructure of the economy, but almost all deplored the way in which the CPP Government tried to implement its policies. Complaints were made of lack of consultation and refusal to make adequate feasibility studies. It was often this as much as ideological disagreement and class antagonism that led to strained relations between politicians and administrators. One CPP minister interviewed pointed out that many civil servants had been keen nationalists themselves before independence. Those who had reached senior posts by the end of CPP rule had in many cases been district officers at the time of the 1954 and 1956 elections and the Togoland referendum and had, according to the Minister, helped to rig these in the party's favour.

Independence had brought rapid promotion for many and the challenge of new areas of state activity. None of the CPP ministers interviewed, even those holding office up to the time of the coup, believed that there had been a worsening of relations with civil servants. Had not the most rebellious officials left the service, leaving behind those who were willing to serve loyally? The CPP view of the administration was of a body that needed a lot of prodding but which, like a properly trained houseboy, could eventually be trusted to do the jobs given to it, once the master had laid down the law.

Civil servants did not accept the rosy picture painted by those who had ruled them. The majority expressed relief that politicians pursuing unworkable policies had been overthrown, even without being specifically asked about this. With the change of government, there was an opportunity for officials to place before their masters recommendations which it had previously been futile or foolhardy to make. If there was a dearth of novel proposals, and members of both the CPP and the military Government often complained that there was, there was certainly no lack of ideas on what the Government ought not to be doing.

In examining the statements of NLC members and civil servants after the coup, it is sometimes difficult to determine who was acting as a spokesman for whom. Were the speeches of NLC members the public expression of views which officials had long wanted to present, or were the statements of officials those of turncoats who were now trying to discredit CPP policies which they had played a major part in formulating? There was plenty of support in Ghana for both interpretations, and they may not be completely incompatible. Civil servants shared with other sections of the community a certain enthusiasm for Nkrumah's policies in the early years, but most had become disillusioned long before the coup. By 1966, uniformed officers and senior civil servants shared with most other sections of the middle class the view that priority should be given to reducing the country's foreign debts, which totalled about £280 million, and that such economic development as conditions allowed should be concentrated on providing basic amenities for rural areas rather than on 'prestige projects' in the towns. General Ankrah criticized the waste of £12 million on Tamale Airport and other prestige projects when there was a need for more dams, irrigation and feeder roads.[15] General Afrifa expressed a similar belief in allocation of more resources to help rural development, and one of his first actions after succeeding Ankrah to the NLC chairmanship was to create a new Ministry of Rural Development. He had earlier promised that the Ministry of Finance would support any effective programme aimed at increasing the supply of good drinking water in rural areas,[16] and his budget for 1968-9, which he described as a 'water budget', almost doubled expenditure on rural water supply. Water now absorbed two-thirds of the development budget spent on rural areas.[17] The Economic Committee had in the previous year (when the majority of its members were still civil servants) suggested the main differences between NLC and CPP development policy. The CPP had ignored the viability of projects, and had concentrated development along the coast, with the emphasis on capital-intensive, publicly-owned enterprises. The NLC favoured viable, labour-intensive projects that would reduce unemployment and would be directed towards 're-orienting productive investment into the rural economy'.[18] Restriction of the state's role to concentration on the infra-structure of the economy appeared to suit both pragmatic soldiers and the non-socialist officials condemned by Nkrumah.

Apart from the broad area of agreement between military men and civil servants on policy, relations between the two were also helped by greater agreement, compared with the CPP period, on the line of demarcation between administrative and political territory. Officials who had served under the CPP were able to list instances of political interference in what they regarded as administrative matters, and of the contempt shown for the administration through by-passing the proper

channels. Ministers decided what sort of food should be given
to political prisoners and, together with regional and district
commissioners, gave instructions to the police on whom to
arrest; Kwesi Armah decided personally to whom import
licences should or should not be granted when he was Minister
of Trade.[19] Those who served at regional and district levels
were able to give examples of interference by regional and
district commissioners in administration. The siting of a new
hospital in Ashanti, the building of a rest-house in a remote
area where Nkrumah happened to have been born, the allocation of market stalls, and decisions on which areas were to be
given priority in the provision of water, electricity and roads
were all said to have been the results of improper 'political
interference' at various times, as was the neglect of towns such
as Hohoe, which had voted against the CPP for as long as free
elections had been permitted.

After the change of government there were some decisions
that the NLC clearly reserved for itself. Just as the CPP decided whom to put in detention and for how long, so the NLC,
in consultation with military and police colleagues, took
decisions on the use of protective custody without asking
civil servants for their views. The disqualification issue was
another on which there appeared to have been no consultation
with civil servants,[20] but beyond these matters, which were
literally questions of life and death for those who had overthrown Nkrumah, officials played some part in the formulation
of most policies. All those interviewed agreed that there was
less 'interference' in what they regarded as administrative decisions than under the previous regime. The extreme view was
that the coup had meant the removal of all political pressure.
Objective criteria could now be used in taking decisions,
whether they involved the allocation of import licences or the
sinking of village wells. NLC members were too busy, and
civilian commissioners too wise, to interfere. A more moderate
view was that interference continued under the NLC but on
a much smaller scale. Members of the Government continued

to interfere with personnel matters in the Civil Service, such as postings, and the appointment of a soldier to chair the Public Services Commission was criticized. One officer was said to have gone out to purchase supplies for his Ministry personally as a result of impatience with 'the proper channels', but this sort of activity declined as NLC members gained experience.

Civil servants who served under NLC members holding portfolios admitted that much of the work normally in ministerial hands was left to principal secretaries, especially between March 1966 and June 1967, when most NLC members were in charge of several ministries in addition to performing their military and police duties. Only one principal secretary openly described the period during which an NLC member headed his ministry as 'disastrous', and this appeared to be due to that member's lack of an adequate understanding of the ministry's problems, rather than to interference in administration. In other cases, civil servants praised the way in which the NLC had coped in a difficult situation, and if General Afrifa felt that officials had been too deeply involved in policy decisions that were beyond their scope,[21] the officials did not complain overmuch about this.

For the most part, uniformed officers and principal secretaries appeared to speak the same language. Despite complaints about instances of slowness or lack of initiative in the Civil Service, the officers had, unlike many civilian politicians, received the sort of training which made them used to a hierarchy in which a certain routine had to be followed, and in which one did not depart from accepted procedures without good reason, although the Civil Service probably took this approach to greater extremes than the army or the police. Even the complaints of Harlley, Kotoka and Ocran about slowness in the Civil Service[22] suggested a certain resignation to the fact that governing a country was more complicated, and probably more frustrating, than running a barracks. Committees might be reorganized and departments merged, but dependence on officials' expertise made it necessary to come to terms with the Civil Service method of approach, just as the passenger might patiently, or perhaps impatiently, allow the driver to follow an apparently roundabout route, due to his own inability to drive or to his unfamiliarity with the locality. General Ocran was one soldier who modified the views he had expressed during the NLC's first year in power. In 1968 he observed that: 'The Civil Servants of Ghana have given us their fullest co-operation and made our work much easier. Only a few have dragged their feet. . . .'[23] In discussing their relations with the NLC, several officials used the identical sentence to describe their masters. Unlike many CPP ministers, 'they were not bullies'. The problems considered in the next chapter may suggest that a bit more 'bullying' might have been in the national interest, but from the point of view of keeping the machinery of government going, as opposed to introducing sweeping innovations, the mutual confidence that the NLC and civil servants had in one another was a great advantage.

How the Machinery Worked

There is no doubt that the inexperience of, and pressure of work on, NLC members left considerable influence in the hands of civil servants. B. D. G. Folson, a university lecturer in politics and a member of one of the few advisory committees which excluded civil servants, described the administrative structure before civilian commissioners were appointed. The NLC committees, composed mainly of civil servants, wielded effective power. All memoranda to the NLC passed through them, thus enabling them to slant their recommendations, which in most cases the NLC approved. It was civil servants who had benefited most from the coup in the short run, and Folson felt that there was a possibility of their attempting to increase their own power by building a wall round the NLC, and keeping it out of touch with public opinion.[24] F. E. Boaten, principal secretary at the Ministry of External Affairs, denied that the

NLC merely approved its committees' recommendations,[25] but critics continued to attribute decisions they disliked to civil servants. The *Daily Graphic* claimed that some civil servants had been deliberately misleading the NLC in order to weaken the Government, and demanded that fewer decisions should be left in civil service hands. The chief information officer at the Ministry of Agriculture criticized this 'unfounded attack on subversion by civil servants'.[26] When the appointment of civilian commissioners to perform ministerial functions was announced, the *Daily Graphic* complained that suggestions for the disbandment of advisory committees had often been opposed by civil servants, and that the original NLC plans had been 'watered down beyond all recognition'[27] – the previous eight committees had been reduced to four 'to streamline advisory channels'.[28] The *Legon Observer* complained of the lack of a long-term economic policy and attributed this to the composition of the Economic Committee.[29] Kwame Bruce blamed 'the economists in the administration' for the lack of an adequate long-term policy.[30] Offering a more detached view, *The Economist* reported that it was not clear whether civil servants created policy or were a drag on recovery, but that there was a feeling outside the bureaucracy that its top ranks were over privileged.[31]

Some of the criticisms of the Civil Service might have been a survival from the Nkrumah era, when it was often safer to criticize an impersonal bureaucracy than the party comrades at the helm, but under the NLC a view appeared to exist that it was unfair to aim too much criticism at the political innocents who comprised the NLC, and that bad decisions could be blamed on bad advice, in the way that the British press might criticize 'the Queen's advisers', rather than the Queen, for cancelling a royal visit to Ruritania. Yet many civil servants were willing to admit that there were important areas of policy in which they usually had the last word. The Administrative Committee, composed entirely of senior civil servants, was able to bring about a drastic reduction in the number of ministries, from thirty-two to eighteen, a recommendation which would have met with far more resistance from a civilian government wanting to dispense patronage; and the Economic Committee was given a virtually free hand in deciding how the problems of inflation, budget deficits and foreign debts, inherited from the previous Government, should be tackled. Within individual ministries it was now possible to reverse policies which officials had long disliked. Thus the Ministry of Agriculture was able to dispose of many unwanted state farms, the Ministry of Education was able to increase the period of secondary education again from four years to five, and the Ministry of Labour was able to end compulsory trade union membership.

By the first anniversary of the coup, the NLC was presiding over a bureaucracy in which morale appeared to be higher than it had been for many years. Civil servants felt that their profession was no longer being attacked by an 'interfering' government and that they were no longer serving politicians whose policies were harmful or impractical, or both. If part of the price to be paid for making civil servants happier was to allow them a wide degree of freedom in policy-making, this did not greatly matter to the NLC in the short term, because it had few objections to the major policies favoured by civil servants; and where it did want to impose its will – as it did when it increased the Defence Estimates at a time of general retrenchment, or when it decided how to punish members of the former regime – it had little difficulty in getting its own way. If they had had to live through the period from February 1966 to February 1967 again, it is doubtful whether those who served in the NLC or the Civil Service would have wanted to arrange things very differently. In the long run, however, the arrangements introduced after the coup had serious weaknesses. Officials might welcome the absence of politicians who 'interfered' with their work, and NLC members might congratulate themselves on following 'expert advice' instead of surrendering to pressure from party comrades, but to govern is to to choose, not merely to administer, and still less to provide a mutual admiration society for civil servants and their masters. Having taken decisions on the problems that most obviously needed attention, such as ensuring its own survival, pruning government expenditure and making plans for civilian rule, the NLC needed some means by which it could 'process' the expert advice coming to it from various quarters, and by which it could decide on priorities when the different proposals were incompatible. It was at this stage that it was felt necessary to bring in civilians from outside the public service.

V : Civilian Recruits

The NLC, like all military governments, was faced with the problem of deciding what sort of civilians, if any, should be allowed to assist it in governing the country, and what sort of roles they should be given. The complete exclusion of civilians, other than civil servants, would have left the Government with inadequate technical knowledge and inadequate contact with many sections of the public, for, as Professor Finer has observed, armies lack the technical ability to rule any but the most primitive community.[1] The inclusion of too many civilians, or the granting of too much power to them, might have left the NLC with inadequate power to follow the policies it felt it had a mission to carry out. Between these extremes, a happy medium had to be sought in which the NLC might be able to benefit from the expertise of various individuals, without feeling inhibited from saying 'No' to them when this was considered necessary.

We have already seen that the main justification given for taking power was that Dr Nkrumah had not permitted the people to change their Government by any other means, but having got rid of a dictatorship, why not allow the people to elect a civilian government as soon as an electoral register could be compiled? The answer usually given was that two conditions should be fulfilled first: the economy had to be rescued from the state to which Nkrumah had reduced it (it was often implied that an elected civilian government might not have the courage to take the tough measures necessary), and the people had to be re-educated in their political rights. General Afrifa stated explicitly that he wanted economic recovery and the familiarization of the people with their rights before the return of civilian rule.[2] General Ocran insisted that party politics should not be permitted until the NLC had laid firm foundations of 'respect for the democratic process,'[3] and Inspector-General Harlley spoke of the need for political education before civilian rule, arguing that a democratic constitution would not alone guarantee democracy.[4] The NLC was to judge when Ghana was 'ready' for democratic civilian government, just as colonial masters had earlier set themselves up as judges of the country's readiness for independence. Until the day of readiness arrived, 'unofficial' members were to be brought into the political process to make it more efficient and more representative.

If it was accepted that civilian assistance should be employed, questions still arose as to what sort of institutions should be created and what sort of functions they should perform. Decisions on these matters appeared to reflect both the NLC's admiration of the British political system, which comes out so clearly in General Afrifa's book justifying the coup,[5] and Ghana's experiences during the later stages of colonial rule. The ideal system appeared to be regarded as one in which a government was answerable to a parliament which would offer constructive criticism, and in which as many channels of communication as possible could be kept open between government and governed. The fact that a presidential system had been tried by Nkrumah was enough to condemn it in the eyes of the NLC. The obvious alternative was to turn to the 'British model', and what emerged might be regarded as either an imitation of the later stages of colonial rule, with bodies created to perform functions similar to those of the executive council and legislative council, acting subject to the vote of NLC, which had collectively taken on the governor's duties, or as an imitation of the 'Westminster model', stripped of such important features as elections and the possession of legislative power by Parliament. The latter imitation might appear to have been so pale as to be unworthy of comparison with the original, but it was General Ankrah, the NLC chairman, who described the National Advisory Committee as being similar to a parliament without legislative power,[6] and the belief that a government could enjoy the benefits of the expertise of politicians without the embarrassment of having to capitulate to some of their demands, is one that requires examination.

Before time could be given to thoughts about the creation of a mock parliament or the allocation of portfolios to civilians, the NLC was faced with the immediate problem of setting machinery in motion to make possible the initiation of new policies in place of the old ones against which the coup had been directed. Four advisory committees were set up immediately on economics, administration, publicity and external affairs. These included only three civilians from outside the Civil Service – the principal of the Institute of Public Administration, the Governor of the Bank of Ghana, and the director of the School of Administration at the University of Ghana[7] – but other committees appointed in the first half of 1966 relied more heavily on 'outsiders'. The Legal Committee, which was charged with recommending the removal of 'all inimical laws which encroached upon the fundamental freedoms and welfare of the people of Ghana',[8] consisted entirely of lawyers, and the Agricultural Committee included six specialist academics and two representatives of the Veterinary Medical Association.[9] Alongside these standing committees, a series of *ad hoc* commissions and committees were appointed to examine particular problems or areas of policy. Apart from the Constitutional and Electoral Commissions, which were looking ahead to civilian rule, the period of military rule saw reports on matters as diverse as the structure of the public services, the running of various state corporations, import licensing, the local purchase of cocoa and the reform of the educational system. All these committees and commissions were useful in ensuring that the expertise of administrators and specialists was available before decisions were taken, and an official publication was able to draw a contrast with the situation before the coup:

A peculiar system of administration was ... developed

which made it possible for the deposed President alone to take important decisions affecting every Government activity at a time of accelerated expansion all round, and reduced the normal organs of administration to mere instruments for the execution of Government policies.

The concentration of political and executive power in the hands of a single individual, and the capricious exercise of this power, eliminated completely from the decision-making process and policy formulation, technical and professsional officers at all levels of administration, thus depriving the nation of the best available use of technical and professional expertise.[10]

Whether this is a fair description or not, it reflects the view held by the NLC and many civil servants that many decisions had been taken by the previous Government without adequate consultation, and that this fault was now being rectified. If the NLC pamphlet exaggerated the extent to which experts had been ignored, there were certainly cases where decisions had been arrived at without consultation, as with the introduction of compulsory primary education in 1961 and the issue of free school textbooks. The NLC description of Nkrumah's administration serves as a reminder of the way in which faith in 'the expert' had increased at the expense of faith in ideology. While the Nkrumah Government obviously did consult experts, few of the public utterances of its members suggested that pressure groups or individuals had useful opinions or knowledge to contribute. The Government urged the need for loyalty to the President and for a study of party ideology, and hoped that all would then be well. If policies were being pursued in the interests of socialism or African unity, criticism was useless, and possibly dangerous for those making it. The NLC, in contrast, showed a healthy contempt for ideology. General Kotoka's observation that terms like socialism meant nothing to him, and that the people simply wanted to be governed properly and honestly, has already been noted. 'They have needs.

Satisfy them: that is all.'[11] If one viewed government as an exercise in 'satisfying people's needs' rather than as part of a grand design for establishing a socialist state, then there was a place for consulting as many experts as were available, subject only to the qualification that they should not have been associated too closely with the previous Government.

The common feature of all the standing committees and commissions and committees of inquiry was that they were all bound by their terms of reference to take a 'partial view' of politics. Apart from the NLC itself, there was no body before June 1966 to take a 'broad' view and to work out ways of co-ordinating the various policies that were being recommended. Politicians were almost completely excluded from the standing committees. Of sixty members only one, the chairman of the Legal Committee, had been active in pre-coup politics. It was in June 1966 that the Political Committee was established:

(i)   To make proposals to the NLC as to what modifications may, in the opinion of the Committee need to be made in any enactment, decision or policy made, taken or adopted by the NLC since the 24th day of February, 1966 so as to make any such enactment, decision or policy serve more closely the public interest and meet legitimate public objections;

(ii) to make such proposals to the NLC as in the opinion of the Political Committee would further safeguard both the interests of the people of Ghana as well as those of the Republic;

(iii) to consider and advise the NLC on such new proposals relating to the policy of the NLC as the Council may submit to the Political Committee for advice thereon, the Political Committee being guided in the performance of this function by the best interests of the people of Ghana as well as those of the Republic;

(iv) to perform such other functions as the NLC may from time to time assign to it.[12]

Thirteen of the committee's original twenty-three members were former Opposition politicians and one (B. A. Bentum) had been a minister under Nkrumah. The 'political animal' was now recognized as having a place in the NLC's scheme of things, but he was to be kept in a separate cage and his function was to be only advisory.

The decision to appoint *ad hoc* advisory committees on matters such as administration and economics was only to be expected. Without such bodies, the military Government would have found it difficult to take or execute any policy decisions. The decision to appoint a Political Committee was more remarkable. It helped to emphasize that, unlike many military governments, the NLC was not anti-politician but only anti-CPP. General Afrifa admitted that a military government was chosen in preference to an appointed civilian one because 'few honest civilian politicians' were available at the time of the coup,[13] but little time was wasted in finding politicians considered sufficiently honest to serve in an advisory capacity. Within a month of the coup, Dr Busia, the former Opposition leader, had returned from exile and announced that he would place at the NLC's disposal what he had learned abroad,[14] and six weeks later members of the Political Committee were informed of their appointments, although these were not made public for another seven weeks. Some cynics felt that the Political Committee was simply a device for keeping former Opposition politicians out of mischief, but the NLC already appeared to have ample means of doing this with the use of protective custody. The alternative explanation is that it genuinely believed that politicians had a useful role to play, although it was not clear exactly how the Political Committee would operate in relation to the other, civil servant-dominated committees, some of whose members were fiercely anti-politician.

The Political Committee's terms of reference were so broad that its members felt they had a right to comment on any policy proposal emanating from any of the other advisory committees, and especially from the Economic Committee.

There was always a certain amount of mutual suspicion between members of the two bodies. Some Political Committee
members felt that while they had suffered imprisonment or
exile under Nkrumah, the civil servants responsible for many
of his policies were now in a position of influence on the Economic Committee, where they refused to recognize the political
implications of the advice they were tendering. Some Economic
Committee members, for their part, saw the Political Committee as a body of largely economically-illiterate men with
improper ambitions for power. The coup had, they felt, removed one group of politicians who failed to take rational
economic decisions, and all the benefits of the change of
Government would be lost if a similar group were allowed too
much influence. The Political Committee was handicapped by
lack of access to the minutes of the Economic Committee, which
made it difficult to find out the basis on which recommendations on economic policy had been made, with the result that
it was usually difficult to get the Economic Committee's
recommendations modified. One exception to the general
rule was said to be the thorough investigation which the Political Committee made of the Inter-Continental Hotels agreement, negotiated by the Economic Committee. It had been
proposed to make an American firm responsible for the management of the Ambassador Hotel and the new Continental
Hotel in Accra, on the grounds that the Ambassador was
making a loss, yet the Political Committee found that the
hotel's accounts had not been audited for five years, and the
evidence they collected from the hotel's managing director
suggested to the committee that it was making a profit. The
agreement was signed despite the Political Committee's
opposition, and the whole episode added strength to its view
that economic policy was too serious to be left to economists,
while Economic Committee members remained satisfied that,
in the vast majority of cases, the NLC took little notice of the
Political Committee's views on economic matters.

The above description suggests that the Economic and

Political Committees were competitive to a greater extent than the NLC might have hoped, but there was also a sense in which the two bodies were complementary. There were many economic matters, such as the re-negotiation of foreign debts and the pruning of public expenditure, on which it was important to take decisions as quickly as possible, but on more specifically 'political' or constitutional matters there was less urgency, although decisions had to be taken eventually if the army were not to remain in power for ever. The Political Committee's major achievements lay in the latter field, where it was able to set in motion the machinery that ultimately brought about the restoration of civilian rule. The whole process gained a momentum it might not otherwise have acquired. The NLC was ready enough to state its desire to relinquish power as soon as possible, but Political Committee members complained that there was no sense of urgency about taking the necessary steps. The Constitutional Commission, promised a few days after the coup, was not appointed for seven months. The civil servants who advised the Government on most matters would have been the last people to press for the speedy election of a new civilian government, bearing in mind their memories of the last one. So it was left to the Political Committee to apply the necessary pressure. It helped to shape the terms of reference of the Constitutional Commission, which in turn led to the election of a Constituent Assembly and the drawing up of a new constitution. Early in 1967 it recommended the appointment of civilian commissioners. The idea was originally rejected by the NLC but, as we shall see, the attempted counter-coup of April 1967 helped to convince NLC members that they could not control the army and police effectively and hold two or three portfolios each. Once the idea of appointing commissioners was accepted, it was the Political Committee that compiled a short list of candidates and made the recommendation that none of its own members should be appointed, thus leaving them free to prepare their own political careers in the Second Republic.

While the various civilian advisory bodies were invaluable in helping to provide the technical and political expertise which the NLC lacked, the problem of deciding how to distribute executive power effectively remained. The problems resulting from leaving too much power with civil servants were discussed in the previous chapter, yet it was impossible for eight NLC members to run eighteen ministries effectively, in addition to their army and police duties. There still appeared to be some who wanted to try, even a year after the coup, and not all officers shared General Ocran's modesty about the limitations of uniformed men in politics,[15] but frustration with the result achieved in relation to the efforts expended would almost certainly have led eventually to attempts to spread the work load. If civilians were not to be given portfolios, the only obvious alternative was to put more army and police officers in political positions. The main difficulty here was that the services did not have an unlimited supply of competent officers. The coup itself had already had the effect of diverting a lot of the highest officers into politics as members of the NLC and the nine regional committees of administration. To divert any more might have weakened the forces seriously. At the beginning of 1967 there were only fifty-two army officers above the rank of captain, and eight of these were removed for political reasons in April.[16] The attempted counter-coup in April 1967 was significant both because a lieutenant came near to toppling a government headed by a lieutenant-general, and because it served as a reminder of how the need to fill political posts had led to a situation where a junior officer was able to command the squadron that marched on the capital. To have given still more political appointments to soldiers might have reduced the army's coherence still further. The case for appointing civilian commissioners, already argued by the Political Committee, in the press and by at least one academic who wrote to General Ankrah personally, was strengthened by the events of April 1967. To make their position more secure against threats of subversion, NLC members needed to devote more time to army and police duties, and the easiest way of doing this was by handing over many of their portfolios to civilian commissioners. Fourteen commissioners were appointed in June 1967 and, together with the seven surviving members of the NLC, they served on a new National Executive Council which was charged with 'the general direction and control of the Government of Ghana'.[17] The NLC, however, retained its monopoly of legislative power, together with the control over appointments which it possessed by virtue of its position as a collective head of state. The Government was still a military/police one, and civilians only enjoyed such power as the military chose to give them. The Political, Legal and Publicity Committees were abolished, and a new National Advisory Committee was appointed whose functions were:

(a) to serve as a forum for the discussion and ventilation of any matter of national importance which may be referred to it by the NLC and offer its advice thereon:

(b) to assist the NLC in the initiation and formulation of any national policy and to endeavour, in assisting the NLC in this regard, as far as possible to ascertain and give expression to public opinion on the said policy:

(c) ... to consider and make recommendations on any subject matter within the competence of any commissioner responsible for any subject or department of State which may be referred to the National Advisory Committee and generally to advise on such other similar matters as in the opinion of the National Advisory Committee ought in the public interest to be submitted to it.[18]

The committee included all fourteen civilian commissioners, together with seventeen members holding no portfolios, nine of whom had been members of the Political Committee. The anomalous situation in which one committee was responsible for a bundle of functions labelled 'political', while others handled 'non-political' matters, such as economics and agriculture was now ended. There was now a forum which, although it possessed no formal powers, enabled the executors of policy and the scrutineers of policy to confront one another, as in 'Westminster-type' parliaments. The results of these institutional changes will be examined after considering the backgrounds of the individuals involved.

The Background of the Recruits

If there are countries where soldiers inhabit remote barracks and have little contact with the civilians on the other side of the barbed wire, Ghana is not one of them. In a small country with a population of less than ten million where only a small minority of people over the age of thirty have received secondary education, the paths of army and police officers invariably cross those of other educated Ghanaians at different times in their lives. The extended family, the district, the school, the church, and social bodies such as the Accra Turf Club, all provided points of contact long before the coup, while the course of business inevitably brought together police officers, who formed half the NLC's membership, and lawyers, who occupied seven of the original twenty-three places on the Political Committee and ten out of thirty-one on the National Advisory Committee. Several of the academics interviewed at the University of Ghana had had acquaintances long before the coup among the officers who subsequently formed the NLC, and academics, too, were well represented on the Political Committee (six members) and the Advisory Committee (nine). All this suggests that as a 'selection committee', the NLC had no lack of knowledge of the civilian talent available, though it was greatly helped in its work by the Political and National Advisory Committees. Apart from compiling a short list of civilian commissioners the Political Committee, like the National Advisory Committee after it, was important in recommending personnel to serve on the many commissions and committees of inquiry. In making the actual selections, there was a need to cast the net widely enough to minimize complaints about tribalism, and to maintain the coup's legitimacy by excluding members of the former regime, except in a few special cases. On the more positive side, those appointed to the Political Committee, the Advisory Committee and the Executive Council appear to have been chosen because they belonged to one or more of four broad categories: specialists, administrators, 'non-political laymen', and politicians. Half of the commissioners appointed in 1967 might be regarded as specialists in the work of the ministries they headed. The Agriculture Commissioner was an agriculturalist, the Economic Commissioner a former Government statistician, the Education Commissioner an academic. Health was headed by a doctor, Justice by a barrister, and Labour by the former Ghana representative at the International Labour Organization. A former town clerk was responsible for Local Government and a former permanent secretary at the Ministry of Trade headed that ministry.[19] Subsequent re-shuffles preserved the specialists' heavy representation, with the appointment of an economist, a former Lands Department official, a company director and two agriculturalists to Economic Affairs, Lands, Trade, Agriculture and Rural Development respectively.

The administrators who served as commissioners overlap to some extent with the experts. Five of the twenty men who held office as commissioners were ex-civil servants, and it is not clear in some cases whether they were chosen mainly for their technical knowledge or their administrative skill. Only one former politician was given a commissionership, and the remaining posts were given to laymen with no political experience. Five of these were lawyers and the other two were accountants. On the major non-executive bodies, the Political Committee and the National Advisory Committee, politicians were better represented. Of the original twenty-three members of the Political Committee, thirteen were former Opposition politicians. In occupational terms, the most prominent groups were the judiciary with seven members and the universities with six. The pattern was not radically different among the Advisory Committee members not holding portfolios: six were politicians, five were academics, and most of the remainder came from the professions, business, the chieftaincy, and the trade unions.[20]

How the New Institutions Functioned

It has been suggested above that the military Government realized that there was a gap that neither it nor its officials could fill in the policy-making process, and that it wanted institutions that would perform 'parliamentary' and 'cabinet-like' functions, but it is not clear what sort of notions the NLC or those it appointed had of what parliaments and cabinets did, or ought to do. The appointment of specialists to various executive and advisory positions, and the appointment of the Political and National Advisory Committees, suggested that the NLC felt secure if it had contacts with both experts and those on the receiving end of policy, before it made a decision. Commissioner of Police Yakubu announced in July 1968 that the ban on political parties was retained on the advice of the National Advisory Committee and that 'As soldiers and policemen we ... think the advice ... is genuine and acceptable',[21] and Commissioner of Police Deku, in justifying the election arrangements to precede civilian rule, similarly took comfort from the fact that the NLC's decision was based on 'good advice'.[22]

The perceptions of those appointed to executive and advisory positions of their functions depended largely on their own backgrounds. Interviews with different members of the National Advisory Committee revealed widely differing pictures of the committee. Some members complained of the frequency with which the NLC ignored its advice; others claimed that 80-90 per cent of its advice was followed. A minority saw the existence of rival 'party factions', which were invisible to the rest. The politician who expected something similar to a parliament sometimes felt cheated when none of the 'parliamentary' checks on the executive could be applied, and it was the chairman, Dr Busia, who complained of actions frequently taken without the committee's knowledge.[23] Other members, whose political activities had previously been confined to working within more limited groups, were more impressed with the opportunity to express opinions on a variety of national issues. The expert's perception was different again. He was frequently concerned with preventing compromises on a few issues he regarded as important, and if he failed, this might colour his view of the committee's achievements as a whole.

In articulating public demands, both the Political and National Advisory Committees were limited, compared with Parliament in the old regime, by the smallness of their membership and the fact that they met behind closed doors. Nkrumah's Parliament had not been a model of democracy, but even in its last year it had raised politically sensitive issues such as import licensing and the shortages that went with it, rising rents and the alleged neglect of particular parts of the country. Backbenchers frequently pressed the Government for action by publicly exposing its shortcomings. The committees could not do this, but they appeared to have two advantages compared with other existing institutions in articulating interests. One was that their members were drawn from all over Ghana, so that they provided a service for those with no contacts in the capital. The other was that, in the words of one member, letters addressed to those not holding portfolios 'were not lost in the bureaucracy' in the way that letters addressed to commissioners, NLC members or civil servants might have been. A group that wanted greater protection for Ghanaian businessmen or assistance for cocoa farmers might have achieved better results by getting a member of the Advisory Committee to raise its problem at meetings attended by commissioners, who could pass their recommendations to the NLC, than by writing to a soldier, policeman, or official in a remote office in Accra. On more parochial issues, too, members claimed some successes, including the improvement of refuse collection in Accra, the removal of several CPP-appointed chiefs, and a reduction in the proportion of Southern children in Northern schools.

The disagreement between Advisory Committee members as to how much influence the committee had has already been noted. Most of the major issues that were subjects of public debate during the committee's period of existence appear to have been discussed, with the exception of defence and security matters. The most optimistic member interviewed believed that the committee was invaluable in taking a broad view of national problems, whereas he felt that civil servants on whom the NLC had leaned heavily during its first sixteen months took a narrow 'departmental' view; hence agreements with foreign firms which did not take into account the implications for the country as a whole. This member reported that NLC decisions on which the committee's advice was followed included the increase in the price of cocoa, the opening of the ports to essential raw materials, the reduction in the importation of luxury goods, and both the original and the modified civilian rule timetables. One can question whether many of these decisions would not have been taken even if there had been no National Advisory Committee. On issues like the price of cocoa and the importation of essential raw materials, there were plenty of individuals and groups with strong views, and these might have triumphed anyway, but there was no organized anti-luxury import-lobby, and it is possible that on this sort of issue the committee was able to add force to the demands of those who thought a change of priorities was desirable. Experience of the outside world, however, suggests that the 'pessimists', who felt that the National Advisory Committee, and the Political Committee before it, were able to do little more than 'push at open doors' in making policy recommendations, may have been right. Outside Ghana, elected parliaments with legislative power have often found it difficult to influence their governments, largely because they lack the resources for obtaining adequate information and formulating policy proposals. For an appointed 'parliament' with no legislative power, meeting in private, the problems must have been much greater. Even on the dismissal of four newspaper editors following their criticism of the Abbott Agreement[24] the National Advisory Committee was unable to persuade the Government either to reinstate them or compensate them, despite the support the committee's views had from many sections of public opinion. If it was impossible to influence a 'political' decision like this, it must have been still more difficult to influence decisions on more complex matters where the expert was considered by the NLC to know best. Yet as a long-term influence, both committees may have a greater claim to a place in Ghanaian history. Both were responsible for recommending the appointment, terms of reference and membership of many of the commissions and committees of inquiry which, in turn, provided the raw material for many policies.[25] On the civilian rule programme, the National Advisory Committee continued to set the pace, as the Political Committee had done earlier, and it was responsible for many of the arrangements surrounding the election of the Constituent Assembly which drew up the new constitution. The committee was disbanded in October 1968, and pessimists pointed out that this made virtually no difference to the way in which the country was governed. They may have been right, but by this time the committee had helped to ensure that the days of military government were numbered. To many members, this achievement overshadowed any disappointments resulting from inability to influence short-term policy.

Civilian Commissioners

In attempting to describe the work of the commissioners who were appointed to perform ministerial functions, one is faced with two major difficulties. One is that we cannot easily disentangle the policy decisions which the commissioners arrived at freely from those that were virtually forced on them by NLC pressure or by the need to follow lines that had been laid down in the first sixteen months of military rule. Certain areas where commissioners did not have much influence suggest themselves. The Defence, Interior and Finance portfolios (but not Economic Affairs) were held by NLC members for most of the period of military rule, thus giving them considerable control over the budget and security matters. The other difficulty is that, unlike members of a party or a completely military government, the commissioners had not all had their outlook and approach moulded by working up through a common institution. There was no common denominator among them until the day they were appointed, and generalizations about the way they functioned cannot easily be made. One might have expected expert commissioners to have had too 'narrow' an approach, former civil servants to have been too concerned with interfering in points of administrative detail, and laymen to have exercised control where they were able to learn the necessary political skills, but interviews with commissioners and with the officials who served under them revealed greater diversity. Some expert commissioners betrayed over-enthusiasm for schemes that were thought technically desirable from their own ministries' points of view, and one official complained that his commissioner looked at the amenities provided by his ministry with a 'professional eye', in terms of what was already available in an area and what was desirable per head of population, without considering sufficiently the influence that transport, communications, and relations with neighbouring areas should have on the final decision. Several officials, however, welcomed the appointment of experts as a means of ensuring that ministries were headed by men who understood their problems and who could argue their cases cogently in the Executive Council. The former civil servants presented an equally diverse picture. Some appear to have been over-concerned with supervising the administrative machine, but others were praised by their officials for having learnt where the line of demarcation between commissioner and official lay. Most of the 'lay' commissioners were lawyers, and they appear to have come nearest to the traditional ministerial function of weighing up the merits of the technical arguments presented to them. While some with no political ambition appear to have kept in the background and interpreted their role as that of 'seeing fair play', others were more positive. One commissioner reported that he and his colleagues quickly found that civil servants 'needed pushing' if government was to work effectively.

One feature that nearly all the commissioners had in common was that, unlike most African politicians, they were in the happy position of being able to walk out of their ministries at a moment's notice and into well-paid jobs in business or the professions. (The only actual resignation on a matter of principle was that of the Information Commissioner, K. G. Osei-Bonsu, following the dismissal by the NLC of the four editors who had criticized the Abott Agreement. This was the only obvious case of the NLC trying to carry out the functions of individual commissioners.) The relative independence of commissioners, plus the fact that they had not built up large clienteles in the process of slowly climbing the political ladder, meant that they had a different sort of relationship with the public from their party political predecessors. Nkrumah's ministers, according to civil servants who had served under them, were frequently forced to make concessions to the clienteles they had built up during their political careers, because failure to do so might have led to these groups pressing for the ministers' removal. Commissioners appointed from outside politics had no such 'hangers on' to exert pressure, beyond the normal network of family and tribal links, business associates and friends. If they were influenced by public opinion, it was, according to both the commissioners and the officials who served them, in a different way. There might have been pressure for greater protection for Ghanaian enterprise, for a higher cocoa price or for more expenditure on feeder roads, the ignoring of which might have led to a greater reluctance on the part of some groups to co-operate with the Government. But the sort of pressure that demanded firm A should be given priority over firm B in the issue of import licences, or that town X should have a hospital rather than town Y, was now less effective because there were fewer sanctions available to those making the demands. Party channels could not be used to press for the commissioner's removal; he had fewer corrupt practices, if any, to be exposed in any campaign against him, and he was not so desperate to cling to office that he would give way to any demand in order to survive. This version may suggest that the commissioners were all saints in comparison with their 'corrupt' predecessors, and may be unfair when the commissioners have not been subject to the same searching inquiries of the assets commissions, but the fact that they were not cogs in a larger party machine does appear to have reduced both the pressures and the temptations that may cause corruption and patronage. Freed from these, it appears to have been easier, within the confines of a policy of retrenchment, to adopt a more detached approach in deciding priorities.

If one looks at the commissioners as a collective group working alongside NLC members on the Executive Council, and not just as heads of ministries, how did their tour of duty compare with that of the professional politicians in power before the coup? Some civil servants could think of nothing that the old politicians had been able to do better than their successors. Was an Executive Council of intelligent men with degrees or professional qualifications not better in every way, they asked, than a Cabinet composed of party hacks who had little education beyond secondary school level? Other officials conceded that something was lacking in the new men, and that was a failure, in some cases, to think in 'national' terms. With one exception, they had never played any part in drafting national manifestos and they had never, before joining the Government, been required to make public speeches on the inter-related importance of different policies. If one looks at the period during which the commissioners held office, and accepts that most of the policy decisions of the period could not have been the work of seven busy army and police officers alone, the policies adopted reveal both the strengths and the limitations of the commissioners. On the credit side, the period saw the smooth transition to civilian rule, the de-centralization of the public service, the shift in emphasis from urban to rural development, and the reservation of certain sectors of the economy for Ghanaians. Whatever the merits or otherwise of these policies, they appear to have been accomplished reasonably smoothly. Against this, there was a tendency in some cases to follow policies which seemed perfectly sound within their own narrow context but which had harmful implications when seen in broader terms. Barely a week after the coup, E. N. Omaboe, the chairman of the Economic Committee and later Economic Commissioner, spoke of the need to reduce unemployment,[26] yet his committee initiated a policy of massive retrenchment that made the achievement of this aim most unlikely. Greater freedom of speech was encouraged, even to the extent of permitting a long television debate on the merits of the Abbott Agreement, already signed with the American pharmaceutical firm. When the criticism continued, the American firm withdrew, and a source of investment which the Government had regarded as essential was lost. On a more minor matter, the importation of free American maize was accepted as a goodwill gesture at a time when local producers were trying to sell their own crop. The extension of freedom posed threats not only to foreign investment, but also to the field of labour relations, and over

200 strikes and lockouts occurred during the three and a half years of military rule,[27] several of which involved violence. The Nkrumah Government's more authoritarian approach had imposed its own priorities. Now there were commissioners who were prepared to accept freedom to strike but did not want inflationary wage increases or delays in production, who wanted to base policy on expert advice but wanted to listen to public opinion, who wanted retrenchment in order to pay the nation's debts but wanted to meet demands in the villages for more roads, drinking water, medical facilities and employment. In some cases the policy framework had been settled before commissioners came on to the scene, and they might be defended on the grounds that the commitments already entered into could not easily have been broken, but these are problems common to many people who inherit positions of political power. The CPP Government had not, of course, provided a model of intelligent political judgement, but its weaknesses had more often been due to 'long-sightedness' than 'short-sightedness'. It had ordered more tractors than there were men to drive them, and more aircraft than there were passengers to ride in them, and built a £10 million conference hall that nobody wanted to use but had hoped, admittedly without thorough examination, that its boldness would eventually be justified. With the NLC and its Executive Council, problems arose due to the apparently unforeseen effects of particular policies.

Conclusion

For the first few months of military rule, decisions on politics, economics and administration were taken by three separate bodies – the NLC, the Economic Committee and the Administrative Committee – with little attempt by one body to involve itself in the decisions of the others. The NLC had the right to reject the recommendations of the committees, or to impose its own policies on them, but it rarely did so. It concentrated on demolishing what it called 'the myth of Nkrumah' by denouncing his policies, locking up his accomplices and projecting a vision of the free and democratic state that was to emerge; the Economic Committee devoted its attention to the problems of foreign debts, inflation and the budget deficit, while the Administrative Committee attempted to streamline the administration by reducing the number of ministries and administrative districts. Each was hacking a separate path through the jungle, and, although they were within shouting distance of each other, their paths seldom converged at this stage. While each had so much undergrowth to clear in its own area, the question of 'co-ordination' hardly arose. As more and more civilians were appointed to specialist advisory committees, commissions of inquiry and the Political Committee, a lot more jungle was cleared. This was to the benefit of the Government, which was now able to see more clearly ahead, but it was also faced with the problem of frequently having to choose which of several imperfect paths to follow. Where politicians rule, making such choices after weighing up all the problems involved is one of their main functions; but in Ghana, politicians only advised, and it was uniformed officers, administrators and technicians who ruled. The exclusion of politicians from office was largely due to their own advice, based on the belief that those appointed would have an unfair advantage over the rest when competition for power in the Second Republic began. Indeed, those enjoying office under the military Government might have wanted to retain it by using their influence to postpone the return of civilian rule.

The most obvious effect of the exclusion of politicians from the executive was the lack of decisiveness in certain areas of policy, often based on a desire to have one's cake and eat it. Thus some politicians might have refused to sign the Abbott Agreement after realizing its implications and the likely public reaction. Others would have signed and then dealt firmly with journalists whose opinions threatened the implementation of the agreement. Few would have signed and

D

then stood idly by as public criticism mounted. In most areas, however, little irreparable damage was done. The administrators, technicians and professional men who ruled Ghana, under the leadership of the NLC, lacked some of the finer political skills, but while they held the fort politicians were left to prepare for the Second Republic. This helped to ensure that the NLC could hasten the return of civilian rule. Any short-term gains that were sacrificed were offset by the advantage of reaching this long-term objective more easily.

VI · Running the Regions

The European visitor to Ghana who ventures no further afield than Accra may feel that he is in just another capital city. The hospitality of the people, the colour and the slogans on the 'mammy' lorries may seem distinctively Ghanaian, but the noise, the bustle and the contrast between wealth and poverty could just as easily be found in many other capital cities of the world. It is only when the visitor follows one of the roads out of Accra that he can see clearly that he is not merely in a civilization that is poorer than his own, but one that is fundamentally different. In the villages, where the majority of the population live, national politics mean very little. Fitch and Oppenheimer conclude their analysis of the downfall of Dr Nkrumah by suggesting that:

> It will be in the forests and savannas, where roads turn into paths and where the sun beats down on thatched-roofed shacks, that Ghana's working classes will join together to prepare the future.[1]

Geoffrey Bing, too, foresees the villages as fertile ground for revolution:

> Once force is met with force any army constructed on a rigid European pattern will go down before the guerillas based in the bush and succoured in the village.[2]

These predictions may eventually prove correct, but such preparations were not in evidence between 1966 and 1969. The people were concerned, as they have been throughout the period since independence, with more mundane matters.

Politics, at this level, are concerned with applying pressure to obtain local amenities, and sometimes employment. A casual conversation with a fellow-passenger on a bus journey through Brong-Ahafo suggested the reason for this. 'Do all your villages in England have tarred roads and piped water?' he asked, and he looked suitably impressed on being told that they had. Here lies a reason for the major difference between politics in a country like Britain, where these basic amenities are available, and one like Ghana where the questions of how easily the citizens of a particular village can market their crops, or how soon disease-bearing water will be replaced with a purer supply, are more important than national issues such as the level of income tax, comprehensive education or the way in which the social services are run.

The NLC, like any other Ghanaian Government, had to decide how to deal with these pressures for amenities when the demand, in terms of expectations, was always greater than the supply of resources available. In this chapter we shall consider the sort of regional administrative structure inherited by the military Government, and then go on to examine the way in which it tried to alter the structure once the party apparatus disappeared.

The NLC's Inheritance

The dissolution of the five regional assemblies in 1959 provided one of the earliest examples of the CPP's determination to refashion the constitution on a more centralized basis. Federalism had been a major issue at the 1956 election, and the CPP had reluctantly compromised with its opponents by agreeing to make a place for regional assemblies in the independence constitution. With independence won, the party no longer felt the need to compromise and it was able to pursue its aim of 'democratic centralism'. As early as November 1957, regional commissioners were appointed as 'representatives of the Government in their regions . . . personally and directly responsible to the Government for the administration of their regions and for seeing that its policy is carried out'.[3] Those appointed, and the district commissioners below them, were all party officials, and the regional commissioners were given ministerial status. The 1960 Republican Constitution hardly mentioned the regions, except to list them by name (Article 6) and to state that each should have a House of Chiefs (Article 49). The arrangement whereby each region and district was administered by a party official appointed by the President continued until the coup.

The picture the CPP liked to give of regional administration was one in which the party, as the chosen instrument of the people, was promoting national development at all levels through its workers. One regional commissioner interviewed felt that his position as a member of a democratically elected party gave him a greater understanding of the people's needs than his military successors. Gone were the days when control was in the hands of 'non-political' civil servants. There were now people in charge who understood and enthusiastically supported the ruling party's policy and who could inspire those below them to action. The first obvious hint that regional commissioners were doing more than inspiring their people to greater efforts came in September 1961 when the commissioners for the Eastern and Central Regions were among those asked to surrender property in excess of the maximum value laid down by the President earlier in the year.[4] One regional commissioner was found after the coup to have earned an unlawful income of over £18,000.[5] The sources included the collection of a 10 per cent commission on contracts, a bribe from a businessman wanting an import licence and a bribe from a man wanting a district commissionership.[6] Similar irregularities on the part of other regional commissioners were revealed after the old order had been overthrown. One who had held office throughout the life of the First Republic was said to have acquired N₵30,000 (about £12,000) illegally.[7] In August 1969, two former regional commissioners of the Volta Region were imprisoned for careless dissipation of public funds, having used N₡5,100 of the Industrial Development Corporation's funds to build a house for a 'party activist'.[8] At district level, several commissioners were removed long before the coup due to corruption or incompetence. Peter Barker has described how Nkrumah left district commissioners 'to their fate . . . as they fell due to embezzlement, and blackmail'.[9]

Elected councillors fared little better. 'Singing and dancing' celebrated the suspension of Kumasi City Council in March 1965, following its failure to produce annual accounts for the previous two years and its misuse of funds, including £37,000 spent on extensions to the chairman's 'bungalow' without the Government's approval.[10] (The 'bungalow' is in fact one of the largest houses in Kumasi and is pointed out to visitors with a mixture of envy and condemnation as an example of how public money used to be spent.) The Council was replaced by an appointed management committee, with a civil servant in the chair, but this did not represent a complete return to the pre-independence form of government, as three of the committee's five members were district commissioners. The fate of the Kumasi Council was similar to that of councils in several other areas. With criticism of authority dangerous at a time when even a district commissioner could have a man detained without trial, there were few restrictions on those who wanted to make money dishonestly, and there was little to guide the councillor on what constituted dishonesty. The Central Government might intervene in cases such as the one in Kumasi, where the activities of councillors were scandalous enough to be an embarrassment to the party, and Dr Nkrumah made a regular practice of moving regional commissioners from one region to another in an attempt to limit their power, but the Government lacked the time, the resources, and possibly the will, to attack all local corruption all the time. After free elections ended, council seats and district commissionerships appear to have been 'bought' from those in higher party positions on many occasions.[11] To have prevented the purchasers from exploiting the positions they acquired might have discouraged future buyers from offering such large bribes to obtain appointments.

Apart from the revelations of both the Nkrumah Government and the commissions of inquiry, civil servants interviewed after the coup offered further damning criticism of regional and district administration under the CPP. The complaint that officials had to work under politicians less educated than themselves was made with even greater force in the regions than in the ministries in Accra. The district commissioners were also less educated than the colonial government agents they had succeeded and they were, according to some civil servants, quite incapable of carrying out their task of supervising local councils' work. Functions that had previously belonged to officials were put in the hands of politicians. Since politicians had only occupied these positions for less than nine years of the country's history, between 1957 and 1966, civil servants gave the impression that the period was a brief aberration in which they had to suffer political interference until the NLC came to rescue them. The interference complained of appeared to involve two types of activity, although officials did not always distinguish between them. One was corruption in the crudest sense, such as allocating market stalls or selling district commissionerships to those offering the highest bribes. The other was the deciding of priorities in order to maximize the political benefit. Civil servants claimed that the change in the proposed siting of an Ashanti hospital, the decision to build a tomato canning factory at Wenchi, many miles from any tomato-growing area, and decisions on the siting of schools or the routing of new roads were made for this reason.

The two types of 'interference' obviously overlap, but the classification is useful because the use of each type tells us something different about the politician responsible. The first suggests that he was greedy (or that his dependants were); the second that he or his colleagues needed to 'buy support' even when the CPP appeared to have all the support that it needed – he could not escape from some form of pressure-group politics. The apparent 'greed' of CPP politicians needs little explanation. As in most tropical African states immediately after independence, the claims of the politician's dependants were strong, the temptations to earn illegal wealth many and the checks on corruption few. There were few conventions to guide the politician as to how he should use his power, or on what constituted corruption, so many used their power to the fullest possible extent in the hope that they would not be discovered. The other characteristics of the politician's position, his need to buy support and to meet pressure-group demands, are interesting in that they serve as a reminder of how far Ghana was from the monolithic one-party state which her leader sometimes pretended existed. One CPP minister admitted that those who were discontented with a regional commissioner on matters such as his handling of a chieftaincy dispute, might take their complaints to Accra, even to the President, and might press for the commissioner's removal. This description was accepted by civil servants. District commissioners occupying a lower position in the party hierarchy were even more vulnerable to such pressure. How far 'interference' went is a matter of dispute. Some officials saw the difference between CPP and NLC as only a matter of degree. Those adversely affected by a decision because their demands or their views were passed over could always attribute the decision to 'political interference'. Thus some felt that the failure to tar the last few miles of the road to Hohoe was due to the town's support for Opposition MP Stephen Antor, but it might equally have been due to lack of funds or administrative inefficiency.

If we try to explain why local pressure could be effective, much of the answer lies in the apparent 'softness' of the ruling party. Despite actions such as the imprisonment of opponents, the dismissal of judges and the deportation of journalists, that sometimes gave the outside world the impression of a ruthless dictatorship, there was seldom the same ruthlessness in imposing the party's will on local communities. In fact, its will was not always clear. The sort of conflicts in which the CPP was involved were often over personalities rather than policy. The removal of chiefs who supported opposition parties began a few months after independence, and Acts passed in 1958 and 1959 enabled the Government to withdraw recognition from chiefs and to seize stool revenue and stool property.[12] In many cases, local action was sufficient to depose anti-CPP chiefs without the Government using its powers, since the enstoolment of a chief who supported the Government was more likely to bring resources into the area concerned. Whatever the political allegiance of the chief, his authority was weakened by the extension of both state and party institutions down to village level. Native courts presided over by chiefs had been abolished before independence and partially elected local councils had been introduced in 1951. One-third of the representation on these went to the chiefs until 1958, when all councillors were to be directly elected. In fact, only one local council seat was contested after 1960, by which time any form of open opposition was dangerous, so that most councillors became CPP nominees.

The extension of the party structure to the local level ended the monopoly that the chiefs had enjoyed as intermediaries between the Government and many of the governed. Chiefs complained after the coup that they had lost not only traditional sources of revenue, but many traditional functions. The gong-gong, which was used to summon the people, was often beaten by a party official, party rallies competed with traditional durbars, party drumming groups competed with those in the chiefs' courts, and village development committees were chaired by party officials, but in many cases there was an overlapping of functions. Chiefs frequently took the chair at party rallies to add weight to the party's authority, and they usually remained the main instrument for articulating local interests. The picture is one of interdependence between the party and traditional authorities. Nkrumah admitted after the coup that he had tried to accomodate the chiefs, despite their non-socialist views.[13] Other countries proclaiming a socialist ideology, such as Guinea and Tanzania, felt no need to make such concessions, which suggests either that Ghanaian people's loyalty to their chiefs was more deeply ingrained than elsewhere, or that the CPP was 'softer' than other nationalist parties. The first reason is of some importance in that the chieftaincy in Ghana has always shown considerable resilience by trimming its sails to different political winds without either capitulating to higher authorities or trying to meet them head-on. The 'softness' of the party also played a part. The reply of CPP members to the question: 'Why did you retain the chieftaincy?' was 'Why not?' The party was nothing if not pragmatic. There seemed to be little to gain from abolishing the chieftaincy, and its abolition would have lost the people's co-operation. The party had never attracted the sort of universal support that its counterparts in Guinea and Tanzania attracted. In the 1956 general election, the last one to be contested before the coup, the CPP won 55 per cent of the votes cast. This represented the support of 32 per cent of the registered electorate and 16·5 per cent of the electorate eligible to register.[14] Large areas in Ashanti, the North and the Volta Region supported the Opposition for as long as they were allowed to, and the majority of the population showed no interest in the ballot box as a means of political expression. Even the Progress Party managed to arouse more enthusiasm than the CPP, when the next contested general election was held in 1969. Although the party had been formed less than five months before polling day, it managed to secure the support of over 25 per cent of the electorate eligible to register.[15] If the CPP was incapable of performing the basic function of getting more than a minute fraction of the population to support it at the polls, there is little to suggest that it had the ability to take on the much more exacting function of maintaining continuous contact between the Government and the people. The chiefs had had generations of experience in doing this, and as long as they did not say or do anything that obviously conflicted with the Government's aims, there seemed to be no harm in retaining them.

Most of the chiefs interviewed reported that they and their colleagues had remained responsible for articulating their subjects' demands throughout the life of the First Republic. Very few people went directly to MPs, district commissioners, councillors or even party officials. For a time, the traditional network of communications had extended to the national level, with opportunities for the presidents of the regional Houses of Chiefs to convey suggestions to the Minister of Local Government, but this procedure was later abandoned, as were many other upward channels of communication throughout the political system. Even then, chiefs remained important in their own areas. Their work sometimes overlapped with that of councillors, in those areas where councils had not been suspended, but, according to the chiefs, party officials who did not hold office in any state institution showed littled interest in taking up people's grievances. Most confined their role to that of providing a supporters' club for the Government. They wore the party's colours, chanted its slogans, attended its rallies and occasionally beat up its opponents, but showed little enthusiasm for the bread and butter side of politics.

Some CPP leaders appeared to believe quite genuinely that, despite the part played by chiefs in securing their subjects' co-operation with the Government, and in articulating their demands, party members still did more than shout from the touchlines. Barely a year before the coup, Kwesi Armah wrote that:

On ... all important questions of policy ... discussion begins at branch level. The arguments, pro and con, move on to the District Executive Committees of the Party, then to the Regional Executive Committees, and from there to the National Executive and the Central Committee. Next the Cabinet gives assent, probably with some modifications and interpretations to ensure the fullest possible consensus of party opinion.'[16]

Other ministers, too, reported that party meetings were held at the local level to the end, with debates on such subjects as the cost of living, shortages of essentials and development. This conflicts with the view of a British observer that by 1965 the party had 'settled into an honourable retirement as a kind of minor government department ruled over by a civil servant'.[17] The writer describes how, up to 1962, nearly 200 members had attended the weekly meetings of Ward 16 in Accra. Then, after the attempts on Nkrumah's life, large gatherings were considered dangerous. Membership dues were no longer collected with the usual efficiency, rallies were not held and the organization was confined to a nucleus of 'fifteen to twenty stalwarts'.[18] It is possible that Accra was untypical. Perhaps, somewhere in the bush, there were groups of earnest men and women meeting under the party flag to discuss the nation's problems, but this is difficult to imagine. The state hierarchy, from the Cabinet down to the village development committee, had absorbed most of the party's ablest members. Would these people have gained any advantage by using the party hierarchy as a means of influencing those above them that could not have been gained by using their position in the state structure, and were there any people outside their ranks with the ability or the inclination to operate the party machinery effectively? Apart from ability and inclination, there was also a need for courage. A CPP official in one regional capital reported that, although monthly ward meetings usually attracted over fifty members, fear of preventive detention discouraged people from discussing national politics. Activities were confined mainly to the nomination of personnel to various offices and the propagation of policies decided by the leadership.

The above discussion suggests that by the eve of the coup, politics in the regions involved a number of institutions whose functions often overlapped, including the central Government, which included all the regional commissioners among its members and which appointed district commissioners to execute its policies, local government, the party and the chieftaincy. This diversity of institutions, which contained people with a variety of backgrounds and a variety of claims to be listened to, provided a framework in which local demands could never be silenced completely. Indeed, many civil servants complained after the coup that too many decisions, on matters such as the allocation of resources for development or the allocation of contracts, were the result of political pressures rather than rational planning. Neither did the apparently centralized political structure prevent regional pressures on the Central Government. Ayeebo Asumda, the Upper Regional Commissioner, was said by civil servants to have been successful in getting an increased allocation of resources to his region. Even anti-CPP chiefs in Brong-Ahafo, another region created after independence, admitted that in return for supporting the party in its struggle against federalists in Ashanti, Brong had been rewarded with a greater share of the national cake, including additional training colleges and five new secondary schools. The Volta Region, in contrast, was said to have suffered as a result of its support for Opposition candidates. Nkrumah mentioned the half-completed textile and knitting factory at Juapong as 'the only industry' sited by the Government in the Volta Region[19] and the *Daily Graphic* mentioned the neglect of Hohoe as an example of what happened to towns that opposed the President.[20]

Administrative Changes After the Coup

A no-party state came into being on the day of the coup. Regional and district commissioners and senior party officials were put in protective custody. Secretaries to the regional commissioners were put in charge of the administration of the regions and the most senior civil servant in each district took over the district's administration.[21] The trappings of military rule were only extended to the regions a month after the coup with the appointment of Regional Committees of Administration. Each consisted of the two most senior members of the army and police in each region outside Accra, together with a senior civil servant.[22] The members of the Greater Accra Regional Committee were chosen directly by the NLC. By this stage the military Government had done the minimum that any such government could do in the circumstances if it was to keep the administrative machine going and keep the politicians' hands off the till. For the remainder of its period in office, questions arose as to how the NLC saw the needs of the regions, how far it saw the structure it had created in the month after the coup as adequate for meeting them and how far it felt further changes were necessary. The refusal to admit civilian politicians into decision-making at the regional level raised questions about the way in which soldiers and policemen either functioned as politicians, or attempted to treat regional problems as 'non-political'.

The NLC's Expectations

General Ankrah outlined the functions of regional committees of administration in March 1966. They were responsible for the maintenance of law and order and overall control of government activity in the regions. They were to advise the Government on public reactions to its policies and inform it of the needs of the people. They were to listen to the advice of regional administrative officers, who were responsible for the execution of the regional committees' decisions, and for day-to-day routine matters affecting the administration of the regions.[23] Two points about this description of functions seem significant. One is the mention of 'the needs of the people', which contrasted with the pronouncements of members of the former Government which normally assumed that the party knew what people's needs were. The other is the absence of any hint that the committees' functions were in any way 'political'.

The use of the word 'administration' in the committees' title suggested that they were not to be concerned with deciding priorities, whereas the CPP had felt it necessary to put no one less than a Cabinet minister in charge of each region. A government publication later in 1966 again put the emphasis on the administrative side of running the regions:

> This new pattern of central and local government adminis-
> tration has led to a measure of de-centralization so essential
> for the efficient functioning of all organs of Administration.
> The establishment of Regional and District Committees of
> Administration has afforded the country an opportunity
> to carry down to the district level the services of knowledge-
> able and experienced administrators in places (*sic*) of in-
> competent party functionaries appointed as Regional and
> District Commissioners under the old regime[24]

If the NLC's hopes were to be realized, Ghanaian politics would have to be conducted in a very different manner compared with the past. For the vast majority of the population, 'national' politics as such has never been a subject of great interest, and no free parliamentary elections have yet brought more than half the adult population out to vote. Political interest has centred far more around the development of individual areas. The CPP, like all other parties, had had to exploit local grievances and local quarrels in order to win many seats in 1954 and 1956.[25] Local battles for scarce resources continued throughout the First Republic, with chiefs, councillors, civil servants, regional and district com-missioners and, to a lesser extent, party officials involved in deciding who should head the queue and who should go away empty-handed. The majority of decisions on the allocation of resources were taken on the basis of 'ad-ministrative criteria', taking into account expected costs and benefits, but in a significant minority of cases bribery, nepo-tism, corruption and intimidation were among the weapons used in attempts to influence decisions. Was all this now to be replaced by a system in which competent administrators, working under the impartial eye of soldiers and policemen, decided how to meet the needs of the various localities? Before attempting to answer this question, the various layers of administration that existed in the regions will be described in the hope of indicating the extent to which different institutions might have been potential targets for political pressure.[26]

In October 1967 it was announced that regional planning committees were to be set up in each region.[27] Each was put under the chairmanship of the regional committee of administration chairman and included members of government agencies in the region, chiefs, and members drawn from the universities, agriculture, business and the professions. The committee was to try to reach a consensus on local needs and objectives. Its functions included the co-ordination of development planning for key sectors of the regional economy; the collection of data on local resources, and the submission of proposals on the utilization of these to the Ministry of Economic Affairs and Ministerial Planning Units; and the quarterly reporting of all development activities in the region to the Ministry of Economic Affairs. This procedure was said to compare favourably with the more centralized planning framework under the CPP, because it allowed for a better utilization of local expertise and the greater involvement on the part of local people.[28]

At the next level of administration, the nine regions had been divided into 161 districts under the CPP. In 1966 the number was reduced to forty-seven.[29] Each was put under the control of a district committee of administration, composed of one police officer and one civil servant, which was responsible for law and order, and for the co-ordination of the work of government departments in the district. Each district included about six local authorities within its boundaries. These were put under the control of local management committees, initially under the chairmanship of civil servants. City and municipal management committees included civil servants and council officials, but the committees of urban and local councils were confined to civil servants, together with one member of the local community.[30] Four months after the coup, there still seemed to be the hope that problems previously treated as political could be tackled in another way. Commissioner of Police Deku, the NLC member responsible for local government, observed that if 'politics' were not introduced into local government administration, there was no reason why trained officials should not help to enhance efficiency.[31] This remark is indicative of both the narrow interpretation which a member of the Government placed on the word 'politics', and of Ghana's experience of the conduct of local affairs. In February 1968 a decree was passed to alter the composition of city and municipal management committees so that each now included seven civil servants, three representatives of traditional councils, and ten members appointed from within the area of the authority.[32] By this time the police officer heading the Ministry of Local Government had been replaced by a civilian commissioner who was a former town clerk. Under the latter's guidance, an attempt had been made to reconcile the desire to keep local government in the hands of trusted administrators with the desire to provide greater contact between the councils and the local population.

The lowest level of administration consisted of town and village development committees. Before the coup these had been monopolized by CPP members. In July 1966 it was decided that chiefs and sub-chiefs should chair these committees, with other members elected by such groups as women, youth, and elders.[33] These committees had few powers but were, according to the chiefs interviewed, important in the execution of self-help projects, and in settling priorities before submitting requests for development to higher authorities.

De-centralization

The most radical change in regional administration during the period of military rule occurred with the decision to de-centralize many areas of administration. The Mills–Odoi Commission was appointed in April 1967 to examine the structure of the public service, and it submitted its report in December 1967.[34] The commission criticized the existing centralization of administration on the grounds that efficiency suffered due to control far from the scene of operations, with even minor decisions taken from the centre. The commission worked on the assumption that government was a single operation, even though carried out by many agencies, and argued that there should be one public service covering the civil service, local government, teaching, the police and prisons. All public services at district level should be administered by district authorities except where technological or security reasons made this undesirable. Regional authorities should similarly be responsible for services most effectively performed at that level, including the running of the larger hospitals, secondary schools, teacher training colleges, nurses' training colleges and major workshops. They should be responsible for approving the district authorities' estimates. Central Government staff at regional level should be transferred to the regional authorities and would work under the instructions of the regional administrative officer.[35] The proposals were, for the most part, designed to meet the nation's need after the restoration of civilian rule, but the NLC accepted most of the recommendations.[36] In June 1969, regional management responsibility was given to the nine civil servants who were secretaries to the regional committees of administration and who were styled regional chief executives. They were responsible for overseeing the detailed execution of functions at regional and district levels, in particular for Agriculture, Education, Health, Local Government, Parks and Gardens, Public Works, Social Welfare and Community Development, but they were precluded from taking decisions which involved questions of policy, technical problems or national plans. Officials of the de-centralized ministries were to work under the regional chief executives instead of their principal secretaries in Accra. Regional management committees were appointed under the chairmanship of the regional chief executive and were composed entirely of civil servants – the regional heads of the de-centralized departments. The committees were to be consulted by the chief executive 'on all matters of substance affecting administrative or programme management in the region'.[37]

There were passages in the report that might have been expected to appeal to the military, such as the assumption that government was a 'single operation' which required a 'rational allocation of functions' and that no one was 'really responsible for policies'.[38] The latter observation echoed the view of General Ocran, quoted in Chapter IV that in his ministries the line of authority was ill-defined and diffuse, and that civil servants often did not know who was responsible for what.[39] The NLC's expectations of the benefits that decentralization would bring seemed broadly similar to those of civil servants. They felt there was an overwhelming case for allowing many decisions to be taken in the regions instead of referring them to over-burdened officials in Accra, and both soldiers and civil servants shared the hope that attempts to settle priorities from the village upwards would reduce the scope for political patronage, since each development in any part of the country had to be justified not only on its own merits, but in relation to the alternative requirements that had to be foregone to make way for it.

The Regions in a No-party State

On the working of regional administration in practice, information was obtained from interviews with members of all nine regional committees of administration and from chiefs who had dealings with them. All the civil servants interviewed expressed approval of the policy of de-centralization. According to a technical officer, the same sort of decisions could be reached as before, but more quickly, with less time wasted in waiting for permission from Accra. Administrative class civil servants felt it was advantageous to have the estimates of the de-centralized ministries incorporated in the regional estimates, since this put the onus on the regions to decide priorities between services competing for funds, such as roads and water, instead of each department submitting its own estimates separately to the Ministry of Finance. Under the previous set-up, it would have been possible for village A to persuade one department that it needed a health centre and another that it needed a new road, while neighbouring village B might fail to get either. Now each village development committee was forced to work out its own priorities instead of producing a long shopping list of amenities it wanted. This was the picture given by both chiefs and civil servants in the regions and both expressed approval of the way in which decisions could now be taken on a more rational basis. Civil servants also pointed to the elimination of much wasteful overlapping between ministries that would eventually occur. Previously, a hospital and a school in the same town might have been given their own electricity plants by separate departments and each might operate with considerable surplus capacity, while the rest of the town relied on oil lamps. Now, according to officials, the problem of electricity supply in the town would be seen as a whole.

In maintaining law and order in the regions, the regional committees' functions did not differ radically from the commissioners' they replaced, except that the greater freedom of expression permitted after the coup sometimes led to violent disturbances, such as the dispute over the control of Kumasi Central Mosque, the chieftaincy dispute at Yendi and several strikes, which the previous Government would probably have nipped in the bud. It was, however, an advantage, from the point of view of maintaining order, to have police officers on the regional committees. Through their contacts with fellow officers in the Government they were sometimes able to obtain more personnel and vehicles, and to establish additional police posts. Where the regional committees appeared to differ from their counterparts in the First Republic was in the role they gave to civil servants, their relations with pressure groups in their regions and their relations with the Central Government.

While the regional committees' law and order functions sometimes got them entangled in chieftaincy, religious and labour disputes, the main local pressures they had to meet were for economic development. The formal channels of communication between the committee and the man in the bush have already been described. The village development committee, under the chairmanship of a chief, could submit development proposals via the district planning committee and the regional planning committee to the regional committee of administration. These proposals had to be considered in competition with proposals from hundreds of other villages and towns in order to decide how resources should be allocated. Critics of the CPP claimed that during its period of office, this sort of competition had often been resolved through corruption, nepotism and political patronage; it had been the 'unofficial' channels that had often been the important ones. Was there not the danger of army and police officers falling prey to the same temptations as their predecessors? It is possible that some irregularities occurred which have not been revealed, but civil servants could indicate nothing more serious than a few cases of interference in civil service postings and in the allocation of officials' bungalows. Like their predecessors, the military men in the regions were not normally allowed to stay at their posts for long. The average tenure of office was fourteen months for the chairman of each regional committee of administration, and twenty-one months for the vice-chairman (the average tenure of the member/secretary was also twenty-one months). Unlike their predecessors, but like the officers who served as members of the NLC, it seems that the army and police officers in the regions were not subject to the same sort of political pressure that forced them to give way to certain demands in order to advance their careers. The CPP had never been able, and probably did not want, to remove the roots that it had in Ghanaian society. The regional and district commissioners frequently acquired large clienteles in the course of their political careers, and even regular postings could not prevent them from relating the demands of various groups to the political gains that might result from satisfying them. With army and police officers the position was different. Not only was their stay in each region short; so too was their incursion into politics. Unless they were involved in some serious administrative blunder, their careers as soldiers or policemen were unlikely to suffer as a result of their activities as temporary regional controllers. It was not possible for discontented elements to go to Accra to press for the officers' removal and, as the vast majority of them had no political ambitions, there was no obvious motive for wanting to win favour with particular sections of the community, apart from bribery, and no evidence of this has come to light.

There were obviously many occasions when regional committees of administration had to take decisions that favoured one group at the expense of another, but civil servants insisted that the decisions arrived at were based on considering rational criteria rather than on favouritism. Thus decisions as to which village should have piped water would take into account the size of population and the expense involved; decisions on where new roads should be built might consider their capacity to increase the volume of crops which could be marketed. Decisions such as these were considered as administrative rather than political, to be settled by civil servants and military officers rather than 'political' regional commissioners.

'Unofficial' pressures on the regional administration continued after the coup and sometimes brought beneficial results to those exerting the pressure, but civil servants gave the impression that this was only in cases where a convincing argument was presented or where demands could be met through improvisation, without disturbing the overall plans already made. The former case was particularly likely to arise when NLC or regional committees of administration members attended durbars, as they frequently did, and were pressed by the chiefs to bring various amenities into the locality. The means of persuasion were varied and often ingenious. Chiefs might present samples of muddy water to show what their subjects were forced to drink, in the absence of a mains supply. Some made casual remarks about the state of the roads during tours in which their guests were bruised as they were bumped along mud tracks, and in other cases communal labour was offered in the hope that the Government would meet this with more money. One argument that frequently aroused sympathy was that 'years of neglect by the CPP must be repaired'. Kibi, the home town of Dr Danquah, was one town that claimed it had been punished for supporting the Opposition leader. Under the NLC it was able to persuade the Government to provide a better water and electricity supply, and to begin the construction of a new road to Accra. Improvisation could be used to deal with a variety of problems, the resolution of which was beyond the capacity of the individual town or village. One regional chief executive was able to meet the demands of a village for a midwife and medical staff at a health centre by finding staff from a neighbouring village to provide part-time assistance; another was able to provide a town with the service of a surveyor to help improve the town's layout.

In relation to the Central Government, all regional committees of administration appear to have been important in transmitting local demands. From the start, monthly meetings were held between the NLC and regional committee chairmen and secretaries. With regional de-centralization, all the regional chief executives were required to meet in Accra to argue the case for their regions' estimates, but less formal lobbying appears to have gone on from a much earlier date. The Brong-Ahafo Regional Committee of Administration was reported to have deplored the delay by officials at the Ministry of Works and Housing in the Sunyani Housing Scheme;[40] the chairman of the Volta committee sent an SOS to General Ocran at the Ministry of Works to request action to deal with the effects of the rising level of the Volta Lake on transport in his region;[41] the State Housing Corporation agreed to build thirty-five houses at Tamale following a request from the Northern regional committee,[42] and that committee was among the bodies which successfully pressed for the resumption of work on Tamale Airfield.[43] The Eastern regional committee was able to persuade the Ghana Water and Sewerage Corporation not to cut off the water supply from three towns that had failed to pay their water rates;[44] the Central regional committee pressed the Ministry of Agriculture for the provision of a breakwater at Mumford;[45] Brong-Ahafo was successful in getting permanent buildings for two secondary schools, and the Western regional committee successfully pressed the case for resuming work on the building of the Axim–Half Assini road.

On the internal workings of regional committees of administration, no written information is available. Before April 1967, most army and police members of each committee had been part-time, and this had left the bulk of the work in the hands of the third member of the trio, the civil servant who held the post of member/secretary. After the attempted counter-coup all soldiers who were committee chairmen were made full-time. This was apparently due to the NLC's fear of the consequences of having officers with too many contacts in both the civil and the military administration, following the suspicion that the officer who headed one of the committees had been involved in the plot. In some regions, such as the East, the vice-chairman was also full-time, if there was no army headquarters in the region for him to command. Most civil servants who were asked how the officers spent the time available to them insisted that it was used properly in representing the Central Government in the region. Extensive tours had to be undertaken, and Government policy had to be explained. A large amount of time was taken up with interviewing pressure-group leaders and individuals with grievances. An example of the work undertaken is provided by the public activities of Colonel Yarboi, the chairman of Ashanti Regional Committee of Administration. Between October 1967 and June 1969 his activities included recommending the prosecution of striking students,[46] explaining policy on de-centralization,[47] suggesting a national disaster fund, urging greater publicity for electoral registration in Kumasi,[48] justifying the coup on the grounds of the need to restore civil liberties,[49] urging the Government to establish more effective road maintenance units,[50] attempting to arbitrate in the Kumasi Central Mosque dispute, complaining of the effect on cocoa distribution of flood damage to roads,[51] persuading cocoa farmers to co-operate with agricultural officers in cutting out diseased trees,[52] explaining Government policy on political activities to chiefs and representatives of political organizations in Kumasi,[53] and urging that chiefs should revive their traditional sources of revenue.[54] Even those chairmen who failed to get their activities reported in the press as frequently as Colonel Yarboi were often kept busy in carrying out their basic functions of dealing with strikes, chieftaincy disputes and student unrest, and maintaining a link between the Government and opinion leaders in the regions. The only obvious clues to the possibility of disharmony at the regional offices were where an officer was posted from a regional committee of administration to a full-time position in the army or police, and at least two such postings appear to have been due to bad relations between the officers concerned and their colleagues, which in turn were due to attempts to by-pass the proper channels of administration, or to what civil servants regarded as 'interference' in their work. One civil servant complained that his regional committee chairman had too much time on his hands after his post had become full-time, with the result that he devoted his energy to such matters as instructing his secretary on administrative matters. Another chairman was reported as having wanted his secretary to refer all administrative matters to him and to have played a part in the taking of decisions on postings and the allocation of civil servants' bungalows, but interviews with civil servants suggest that these cases were exceptional. Officials working under army and police officers in the regions, like their counterparts working under uniformed men in Accra, generally expressed approval of the way in which their bosses conducted themselves in comparison with the regional commissioners who had preceded them. Most of them, according to their officials' accounts, concentrated on deciding priorities rather than interfering in administration. They took the final decision in the regions on matters such as which villages should be given piped water or whether a cement factory should be built in a particular town, but even on matters such as these, officials suggested that the final decision was usually the result of recommendations, based on rational criteria, made by regional planning committees, rather than the result of political intrigue.

On the basis of an admittedly small sample, police officers seem to have met with greater approval among civil servants than army officers. No direct questions were asked on the relative merits of the two, but the officers who came in for the greatest criticism were usually soldiers. The difference may have been due partly to age and experience. Even on the NLC, the average of the four army officers at the time of the coup was under forty, compared with an average age of nearly forty-five in the case of the four police officers. In the regions, most of the army officers were younger still, whereas officers of equivalent rank in the police force, which had been Africanized much earlier, were usually older. J. M. Kporvie was fifty-seven when he was appointed chairman of the Northern Regional Committee of Administration in 1966, and Assistant Commissioner of Police S.Q. Archampong had been in the police for over thirty years when he was appointed vice-chairman of Ashanti

Regional Committee in 1968. The army had no one of comparable age. Even General Ankrah, its most senior member, was only fifty at the time of the coup. Apart from age, police officers appear to have gained more of the sort of experience that might have been useful in acting as the regional arms of the Government. The 'maintenance of law and order' function came naturally to them, and the nature of police work as an essential part of the day-to-day running of the country had put their talents as leaders of men to the test. The army officers, in contrast, had generally been underemployed, as peacetime soldiers usually are, and few, apart from those who had served under the United Nations in the Congo, had had their qualities of leadership, let alone their political qualities, put to any practical test.

Local Government under the NLC

It seems to have been at the lowest levels that the military Government's attempts to stamp out corruption were least effective. Koforidua Municipal Council lost N₵5,030 (over £2,000) between December 1966 and February 1968 due to misappropriation of funds by six officials.[55] The Auditor General's Report for the first full accounting year after the coup, 1966–7, was not published until 1970, and it did not suggest any great increase in honesty in local government. It deplored the councils' accounting systems and noted that many rate collection books vanished, possibly for illegal collections. The only revenue official of Jomoro Local Council misappropriated N₵2,085·67, and was believed to have fled to the Ivory Coast. Kumasi City Council was remarkable for 'the regularity of cases of embezzlement of funds by its officials'.[56] The report admitted that, while low standards of accounting might have contributed to some irregularities,

one cannot but conclude from the available evidence that fraudulent practices were in some cases premeditated, and that the successful perpetration of these acts was due not only to inadequate financial control by those in authority but also to the general low moral standards in financial accountability. [57]

At this level, the absence of adequate accounting may always have been as great a reason as party patronage for corruption. At higher levels, the NLC appears to have eliminated much corruption by appointing to high office people who expected to serve only temporarily before returning to their careers in the army, the police, business, and the professions, and who had no 'debts' to pay to 'clienteles' that had helped their political advancement. At the local level, the contrast between pre- and post-coup politics did not appear so great. Elected councillors had disappeared from the scene in many areas as a result of their corrupt activities, long before the coup. Control passed into the hands of appointed management committees. Such committees continued to function after the coup, and although their membership was changed to remove some of those whose loyalty to the new regime was in doubt, the actual practice of local government does not appear to have altered radically.

Conclusion

The regional structure which the NLC inherited had been created by politicians dedicated to building a socialist state, but whose practical knowledge of government was based mainly on what they had seen of colonial rule. Politicians were appointed as regional and district commissioners to perform functions broadly similar to those that had been performed by colonial civil servants, but their lower educational qualifications, their inexperience, and their relationship with the ruling party and the wider community made them victims (or beneficiaries, if they were not caught) of widespread corruption, and of various political cross currents which frequently led to resources being diverted for purposes which, by any standards, failed to give the people of Ghana the benefits that the country was economically capable of attaining. There was, however, the advantage from the point of view of policy-making, that all regional commissioners were members of the Cabinet and were able to exert greater direct influence on Central Government decisions than the regional committees of administration, which only met the NLC monthly, and were therefore less involved in the early stages of policy formulation. The Western regional commissioner, representing the region in which most labour in mining, manufacturing, and transport was employed, was able to participate in Cabinet discussions on the form which the 1958 Industrial Relations Bill should take: the Upper regional commissioner was able to provide Bolgatanga with impressive-looking buildings for the Ghana Commercial Bank and Government Transport. The machinery for intelligent co-ordination of policies between the regions was there, although many of the potential advantages were lost as a result of the pressures described earlier in this chapter, or because of insistence from above on 'prestige spending' in Greater Accra.

The NLC's immediate task was to keep the machinery of government going, and the nature of military rule required that it should put army and police officers in charge of the regions and districts, in place of party politicians. As many of these uniformed officers only held their political posts part-time during the first year of military rule, it was left to civil servants to take many major decisions, and to deal with many pressure groups. These officials and their military masters were not caught up in the sort of game of 'snakes and ladders' that had affected the previous regional and district commissioners, in which one move might have put undreamt of wealth within their grasp, while another might have landed them in preventive detention. The absence of these pressures appears to have made a more rational and honest decision-making process possible, in which attempts were made to deal with competing demands on their merits. With a few exceptions, the process appears to have continued smoothly even after more chairmanships of regional committees of administration were made full-time.

Apart from re-shaping the administration of the regions in order to fill the gaps created by the destruction of the CPP, the main innovation during the period of military rule was the de-centralization of much administrative work to the regions. The proposals on which this policy was based came from a civilian commission of inquiry and, although they met with some resistance from the senior civil servants serving on the NLC Administrative Committee, they proved acceptable to the military Government, apparently because it felt they would end much of the time-wasting activity in which they felt administrators in Accra were involved, without in any way hampering the Government's basic aim of restoring civilian rule under a group of politicians different from that from which it had taken power. The implementation of the de-centralization policy only began a few months before the ending of military rule, but it appeared to meet with the approval of civil servants in the regions who felt that it enabled them to take a broader view of their regions' problems, before submitting recommendations on priorities to the uniformed officers above them.

The cordial relationship which existed between those at the head of the army, the police and the Civil Service, due partly to a mutual dislike of the CPP and partly to the common experience of belonging to disciplined professions, was noted in Chapter IV. This relationship extended to the regional level. As a result, the handicaps from which the uniformed officers suffered because of their remoteness from the public, compared with the regional commissioners who preceded them, were largely offset by the advantages of more harmonious relations with officials. At the same time, traditional rulers generally welcomed the replacement of regional commissioners by the uniformed officers, because the latter represented a government more sympathetic to the institution of the chieftaincy. Enjoying the support of the two important pillars of the Civil Service and the chieftaincy, the regional committees of administration were able to carry out the military Government's will in the regions by relying mainly on civilian co-operation. Only in exceptional cases was a show of force necessary.

THE STRUCTURE OF REGIONAL AND LOCAL ADMINISTRATION*

Regional Planning Committees
Composition: Regional Committee of Administration Chairman, civil servants, specialists.

Functions: To examine requests from towns and villages, work out priorities in development.

9 Regional Committees of Administration
Composition: One army officer, one police officer, one civil servant,

Functions: Representation of Central Government in the regions; execution of Central Government policy: internal security.

Regional Management Committees (from June 1969)
Composition: Secretary of the Regional Committee of Administration (in the chair); regional heads of de-centralized departments.

Functions: To advise chairman on matters affecting administrative and programme management in the region.

District Planning Committees
Composition: Civil servants.

Functions: Recommendations on priorities within districts.

47 District Committees of Administration
Composition: One police officer, one civil servant.

Functions: Law and order; co-ordination of work of Government Departments in districts.

Urban and Local Councils
Composition: Controlled by Management Committees – civil servants plus one member of the local community.

Functions: Running of local government services, under the supervision of Regional Committees of Administration.

City and Municipal Councils
Composition: Management Committees originally composed of civil servants, council officials and one member of the local community. From February 1968: 7 civil servants, 3 representatives of traditional councils, 10 members of local community.

Functions: Running of local government services under supervision of Ministry of Local Government. (Regional Committee of Administration kept informed of activities.)

Town and Village Development Committees
Composition: Chaired by chiefs and sub-chiefs. Members elected by local groups, *e.g.* women, youth.

Functions: Representation of town and village interests, especially in dealing with urban and local councils.

* See pp. 99–104.

VII · The Road back to Barracks

Almost all military governments express a desire to hand over power to civilians as soon as conditions are ripe. How easily they are able to do so depends on the strength of their motives for disengagement and the magnitude of the difficulties in their way. The motives may be both positive and negative. The positive include a genuine belief in the virtues of democratic government and in the greater ability of civilians, compared with soldiers, as politicians. The negative include fears of a split in the senior ranks if power is held for too long, and a fear that soldiers will become so engulfed in political problems that they may lose their integrity and become barely distinguishable from the civilians they originally displaced. Either of these situations could give rise to a counter-coup. Professor Finer has laid much emphasis on these negative motives. He suggests that the decision to return to civilian rule is usually the culmination of three conditions: the disintegration of the original conspiratorial group, a growing divergence of interests between the junta of rulers and the military who actively run the forces and the political difficulties of the regime.[1] In the case of Burma, L. W. Pye describes how the Burmese army returned the Government to civilians in 1960 after finding how difficult governing was. It feared opposition, a loss of integrity and a split in its own ranks if it stayed in power.[2]

The positive motives are less well documented. Many soldiers, like civilians, believe in liberal democracy, not merely as an end in itself but because of their expectations of the benefits it will bring them, but there is, nonetheless, a distinction between those who say to potential successor regimes 'Yes, if' and those who say 'No, unless'. The first type may not be unduly concerned about the nature of their successors' policies, as long as the military are allowed to return to barracks un-molested, while the latter may feel, like Colonel Nasser in Egypt, that they have a mission to fulfil, and that civilians should only be given power if it seems likely that they can carry out the mission better than the soldiers. The 'Yes, if' group often see themselves as constitutional mechanics who hold power only for as long as it takes to repair defects in the political system, such as excessive corruption or the privileged position of one tribe, while the 'No, unless' group may regard themselves as social engineers who have a duty to stay in power to achieve a long-term objective such as 'socialism' or the 'ending of foreign domination'.

The difficulties in the way of restoring civilian rule may be many. Officers who take power often find themselves in the position of the Aborigine who was happy when he received a new boomerang for his birthday, until he found that it was impossible to throw the old one away. The frequent alterna-tions between military and civilian rule in Dahomey during the 1960s showed the regularity with which the boomerang might return. The most obvious problem is to prevent the emergence of a government that might threaten the lives or liberty of the soldiers who have handed over power, and this danger is especially great if control passes into the hands of the politicians the soldiers originally deposed. Apart from fears for their own personal safety, the military may fear the election of any successor government which reverses its own policies or returns to the policies of the previous regime, because this might take the wheel full circle and create conditions favourable for another coup. At best, the former military rulers might then find themselves back in power, conducting the same repairs to the political machine as they had undertaken only a few years earlier. At worst, they might find themselves pushed aside by subordinate officers eager to show their ability to 'liberate the nation'. Additional problems may be created by civilians. While some of these will be keen to see the army back in barracks as soon as possible so that they can take over power, the

E

pressures are not necessarily in only one direction. Some civilians may feel they have more to gain than to lose by the continuation of military rule. Civil servants may welcome the absence of 'arrogant' professional politicians taking 'irrational' decisions as a result of 'improper' pressures, traditional rulers may welcome the increase in their influence as a result of the banning of political parties, and even some politicians may be contented with the continuation of military rule, if they can gain positions of power or influence by negotiating with the soldiers. Pressure groups, including foreign businesses, may feel that they are getting a better deal from a military government than they are likely to obtain from a civilian one, and they may use such influence as they possess to persuade the army to delay the return to barracks. Fearing the consequences of handing over power, and flattered by those who insist, sometimes out of self interest, that the army's continued presence will benefit the nation, a military government may be persuaded to prolong its tenure of office.

Having examined the problems of disengagement in general terms we can now turn to what happened in Ghana between 1966 and 1969. We shall consider the hopes and fears that the prospect of civilian rule held out both for the NLC and the rest of the community, the sort of pressures and counter-pressures that resulted from these expectations, and the civilian rule timetable which eventually emerged.

NLC Hopes and Fears

The actions and words of NLC members suggest that they had a positive belief in the superiority of democratic civilian rule over military rule. Within three days of the coup the NLC announced its intention to appoint a constitutional commission and to hand over power to a 'duly-constituted civilian government, as soon as possible'.[3] There was never any public suggestion that the NLC should stay in power indefinitely, or even that it should try to establish a political movement to sustain it, as was the case in Nasser's Egypt and Mobutu's Congo. Political power was a burden to be borne for as short a time as possible, since soldiers and policemen were unsuited to performing political tasks and had only taken power because there had been no other way of removing Nkrumah. The idea of the army as the people's last line of defence against Nkrumah was one of the underlying themes of General Afrifa's book. He concludes with these words:

> The aim of the unconstitutional military action we took is to regain this freedom and to create the conditions and atmosphere in which true democracy can thrive. This is our defence.[4]

The apparent humility of the NLC, and its desire to be surrounded by wise civilian advisers rather than to insist that it knew best how to govern the country, have been discussed in earlier chapters. In the classification suggested earlier, the men who ruled Ghana were constitutional mechanics rather than social engineers. Even if it could have been guaranteed that they would be able to stay in power for ten years, without any risk of internal dissension and with no threats to their survival from impatient civilian politicians or from subordinate officers capable of staging counter-coups, it is unlikely that they would have wanted to remain in office. In fact, the NLC shared the problem common to many military governments once the initial enthusiasm for the coup had waned. Professor Finer's generalizations about the problems that hasten the return to barracks appear to fit the particular case of Ghana.

The disintegration of the original conspiratorial group could be said to have begun with the assassination of General Kotoka in April 1967. This was said to have left General Afrifa, the other main architect of the coup, out on a limb, with frequent disagreements between him and the rest of the NLC.[5] General Ankrah's resignation in April 1969, after his collection of funds in an attempt to secure his own political future (see below), and

Nunoo's dismissal following arguments about which politicians were involved in the Ankrah affair, could be interpreted as a continuation of the process. The 1967 attempted counter-coup was an obvious symptom of a divergence of interests between the NLC and at least some full-time soldiers; and political difficulties could be regarded as growing more serious as the NLC's period of office continued, while many of the problems originally attributed to Nkrumah persisted.

After three years in power, most NLC members entertained high hopes of what a return to civilian rule would bring. They would enjoy the credit for liberating the nation from dictatorship and for restoring democracy, without having outstayed their welcome or acquired too many of the vices of politicians who often outstay theirs, but for much of the period between 1966 and 1969 there were fears as well as hopes. These affected both the pace and the nature of the process of demilitarization.

The NLC's attitude towards giving up power was usually one of 'Yes, if' rather than 'No, unless'. The conditions most frequently stated, as we saw in Chapter V, were that economic recovery and the re-education of the people in their political rights should precede civilian rule. Behind these conditions were three unspoken assumptions: lack of political education might lead the people to elect a government similar to the CPP, which would threaten the freedom and lives of NLC members; the transfer of power to a civilian government without economic stability having been achieved might make the new regime vulnerable to another coup; and the transitional period leading up to civilian rule might, if begun prematurely, allow the CPP to regain power unconstitutionally as the military Government relaxed its guard. The fear of the CPP's return, however unjustified, never really abated. Even during the last few months of military rule, Air Marshal Otu was in court on charges of plotting to restore Nkrumah, and decrees were still being passed to disqualify members of the former regime from office (see below).

The NLC's concern with economic recovery was partly due to

a fear that failure in this field might reduce the life expectancy of any successor regime and would thus bring the military back into politics, but on this issue, as on that of restoring democratic rights, the matter was not simply one of self interest. Military governments, like civilian ones, often want to be remembered for their achievements and do not like the thought of their successors destroying what they have built. Many civilian governments have no choice in the matter, if the verdict of the electorate goes against them at the end of their allotted span, and they cannot complain that 'We weren't ready to hand over'. Military governments are less restricted and they may judge for themselves when their task is completed. If the NLC's hopes of what civilian rule would bring eventually proved stronger than its fears, the fears were sufficient to ensure that there was no capitulation to those who demanded a quick return to barracks. Dr Busia's demand, barely a year after the coup, for an early election to enable Ghana to convince the outside world that it had rejected Nkrumah's policies and could choose a government that would 'tackle the country's economic and administrative problems',[6] fell on deaf ears. He had to wait for over two more years before the people were allowed to make the choice for which he had hoped.

Civilian Hopes and Fears

Dr Busia's call for an early election was only to be expected. Having led the Opposition to Dr Nkrumah before going into exile, he had a strong claim as heir to the political kingdom and was impatient with the regency which was temporarily in command. Long before political parties were legalized again in May 1969, Busia was generally acknowledged as the leader of a group of politicians whose most distinctive features were business, professional or traditional background and, in most cases, an impeccable record of opposition to Nkrumah. Many proudly displayed the battle scars of exile or preventive detention, and their hopes were that a Second Republic would enable

Ghana to make a fresh start, under men who had suffered for their views and had been proved right by events. This idea of a rebirth was epitomized by the decision of Dr Busia's Progress Party to choose as its emblem a sun rising from a black background, representing a new dawn after the dark night through which the country had passed under the CPP. The men who wore this emblem had no doubt about either their right or their ability to take over as soon as the NLC could be persuaded to step down.

Not all civilians shared Dr Busia's eagerness for an early return to barracks, either because they did not share his conviction that he was sure to defeat any electoral challenge from the rump of the CPP, or because they were fearful of a return to what they saw as the political malpractices of the First Republic, whichever party gained power. K. Nortey wrote of the danger of holding elections too soon in view of the indoctrination to which young people born in the 1940s had been subjected,[7] and G. Adlai-Mortty, the Special Commissioner for Re-deployment of Labour, wrote of the dangers of a multi-party system and increased corruption.[8] William Gutteridge suggested one influential section of opinion that might have wanted to slow down the civilian rule programme. He argued that the successful functioning of ministries under civilian commissioners (only one of whom was a politician) had created a vested interest among many senior civil servants 'in the continuance of a disciplined order'.[9] The description in Chapter V of the Economic Committee's attitude to politicians fits in with this view, and in the regions, too, civil servants showed little enthusiasm for the prospect of politicians once again breathing down their necks.

Outside the ranks of would-be politicians and civil servants, the state of public opinion was more difficult to gauge. Traditional rulers might have been expected to favour the perpetuation of military rule for as long as possible, in view of the way in which their power and influence had been increased,[10] but most of them were shrewd enough to realize that civilian rule must come eventually, and that their interests would best be served by trying to secure a constitution that would protect the gains they had made under the NLC. Businessmen, too, were happy to allow civilians to return, on the assumption that the good relations they enjoyed with the military Government would continue under a successor regime, especially once it was clear that no socialist politicians would be competing for power. As far as the rest of the population were concerned, there appeared to be no strong pressures for or against disengagement. For what it is worth, an opinion poll conducted in late 1967 found that 70 per cent of Ghanaians wanted civilian rule by 1970,[11] but there were no obvious signs of discontent with the NLC among the mass of the people.

It is doubtful whether such hopes and fears as civilians had in their minds had any influence on the decision to return to barracks, comparable with the influence of the hopes and fears of the NLC. In other words, the NLC departed when it felt the moment was opportune. Different civilians might have felt that the moment was either too soon or too late, but there were few direct pressures they could exert to get their way. Those who favoured delay could do no more than warn the NLC that its task of achieving economic recovery and political education were not yet completed. Those who wanted to accelerate the pace were in a slightly stronger position, because they managed to set the right sort of wheels in motion during the first few months of military rule. The Political Committee, as we saw in Chapter III, was able to hasten the appointment of the Constitutional Commission, which was in turn able to bring about the creation of the Constituent Assembly to promulgate the new constitution. There is no reason why the NLC could not have brought these processes to a halt at any stage, but having committed itself to giving up power even before the end of its first week in office, the politicians' task was to persuade it to keep its word rather than to change its mind. The relationship was like that of a bride enthusiastically making the wedding arrangements as soon as the suitor had asked for her hand. The enthusiasm was so great, and the arrangements so elaborate, that it would have been extremely embarrassing for the groom to have to make an excuse for backing out. The NLC had the right to back out, since no government can be sued for breach of promise, but given its 'Yes, if' attitude, the right would not have been exercised unless there had been a very good reason.

Milestones

The NLC insisted that certain objectives should be achieved in both the political and economic fields before it returned to barracks. The economic achievements were more capable of objective measurement, and judged by its own standards the NLC had made considerable progress in the direction of economic recovery by 1969. The balance of payments deficit of nearly N₵200 million in 1965[12] was reduced to N₵128·7 million in 1966 and N₵48·3 million in 1968, with a surplus anticipated for 1969.[13] Foreign debts were re-scheduled so that 80 per cent of the debts due by 1968 were deferred until the period 1974–82.[14] The original (CPP) Estimates of government expenditure for 1966 were cut by nearly 18 per cent by the NLC, and in the following year development expenditure was nearly halved.[15] A budget surplus of N₵3·8 million was achieved by 1967–8.[16] The state enterprises that had existed at the time of the coup, most of which made a loss, had been reduced to forty-seven by 1969, largely through amalgamations.[17] Against these achievements, General Ankrah admitted by the third anniversary of the coup that poor results had been achieved in agricultural production and in attempts to reduce unemployment.[18] The general opinion of the NLC, nonetheless, appeared to be that the economy had been steered away from the disastrous course set by Nkrumah, and that it was safe by 1969 for new men to take over the helm. This appeared to be Afrifa's view when he made his first broadcast as NLC chairman on 8 April 1969.[19]

Political education could not be put to the same objective

tests as economic achievement. If the NLC was sincere in wanting to establish a liberal democracy, two inter-related requirements seemed important. One was to prevent those responsible for what was regarded as the abuse of power under Nkrumah from returning, on the assumption that they might abuse it again. The other was the more difficult one of 'educating the people' in the hope that electors would learn to stand up for their rights, and that those elected would recognize their duties. The function of political education was entrusted largely to the Centre for Civic Education, an autonomous body set up by the Government. Inaugurating the Centre in June 1967, General Ankrah announced that it would provide education in democratic rights and responsibilities, and in the ideals of public service, integrity, and tolerance.[20] Branches of the Centre were opened throughout the country and the *1969 Ghana Year Book* reported that its activities had been programmed in three stages: 'Human Rights in our Community', 'Your Rights and Duties under Your Constitution' and 'The Voter, the Candidate and Parliament'. The last two stages were to be reached once the new constitution had been promulgated.[21] The NLC seemed satisfied that the people had been familiarized with the principles of democracy, but the problems remained of how they were to gain experience in the pratcice of it.

Krobo Edusei favoured socialism when he was a minister under Nkrumah because, in his interpretation, it did not mean giving up what you already possessed. General Kotoka stated that the rule of law was the NLC's aim, 'not the way we are ruling now'.[22] Part of the military Government's message, like that of its predecessor, appeared to be 'Do as I say, don't do as I do'. This is not to charge the NLC with hypocrisy but merely to point out the difficulty in bridging the gap between the ideal of democratic government and the concentration of power, sometimes used in an arbitrary manner, that military rule involved.

After February 1966 Ghana was concerned with tackling

political problems at two levels. There was the problem of
day-to-day government, which included completing the
demolition of the CPP edifice, and there was the problem of
laying the foundations of a new political system to follow the
ending of military rule. The first problem might obviously be
regarded as within the province of the NLC. One can accept,
with Kotoka, that there is no reason for a military government
to pretend to behave like a democratic civilian one, and that in
order to stay in power it may have to ignore democratic
procedures. The placing of CPP officials in protective custody,
or even the parading of one of Nkrumah's 'security men' in a
cage[23] or the public execution of two counter-coup leaders,
were defended implicitly on the grounds that the end of staying
in power, until free elections could be held, justified the means.

The early stages of the transition back to civilian rule
appeared to be relatively smooth. Commissions and committees of inquiry were set up to examine the activities of the
former rulers, and most of those not found guilty of breaking the
law had been released from protective custody by the end of
1968. The Constitutional Commission was appointed in
September 1966 and reported in January 1968. Its proposals
were considered by a Constituent Assembly elected in December
1968.[24] Civilian commissioners with ministerial powers were
appointed in June 1967.[25] Local government was put in the
hands of management committees, consisting mainly of officials,
soon after the coup,[26] and the non-official element on these was
increased in February 1968.[27] Civilian advisory committees on
economics, administration, publicity and foreign affairs were
appointed immediately after the coup[28] and a political committee was appointed in June 1966.[29] By 1969 civilians were
actively involved in the government of the country at national
and local levels, though subject to the veto of the NLC, but
the problems remained of the transition from officers appointed
by the NLC to officers elected by the people.

The election of the Constituent Assembly was itself a subject
of controversy. The original intention had been to elect it by

universal suffrage before the lifting of the ban on political parties. A new constitution would have been promulgated by the NLC after the Assembly had completed its study of the Constitutional Commission's proposals, and only then would the ban have been lifted. General Ankrah justified the exclusion of parties on the grounds that there was a need for the 'dispassionate consideration of the constitutional proposals free from the sectional interests of party politics'.[30] Commissioner of Police Yakubu added that political pressure in the Constituent Assembly should be avoided. There was a danger of one group drowning the views of minorities. Critics complained of both the administrative problems and expense involved in holding two elections, one for the Constituent Assembly and one for the new civilian government, and of the short time interval allowed between the formation of parties and the return of civilian rule. Victor Owusu, the Attorney-General, argued the case for holding only one election with parties permitted, although even he was against an immediate lifting of the ban on parties, due to the need to avoid violence while the police were under strength.[31] Harlley, too, was concerned about raising the strength of the police to contain violence,[32] a possible indication of the NLC's expectations of what party politics might bring.

The decision to hold two direct elections was reversed in September 1968 due to difficulties in getting electoral registration completed in time. It was decided instead to hold indirect elections to the Constituent Assembly through local authorities and institutions in December 1968.[33] The administrative difficulties involved in electoral registration were real enough, but the decision appeared to be in keeping with the NLC's preference (noted in Chapter III) for allowing people to express their views through interest groups rather than 'mass' organizations. Lawyers, trade unionists, civil servants, businessmen, chiefs, midwives, religious bodies and students could elect their representatives to the Assembly, without party politicians touring the country and applying their own kind of pressure for winning votes. No Assembly majority elected by universal suffrage would be able to claim that it, and not the NLC, represented the popular will and should have the final decision in approving the new constitution.

One of the most difficult issues facing both the NLC and the Constituent Assembly in paving the way for civilian rule was that of deciding whom to disqualify from office. If it was believed that a small minority of the population might capture the reins of power, impose a one-party dictatorship on the people and arrest the NLC, how did one go about identifying this group and keeping it out of office? The Constitutional Commission, as befitted a body on which one-third of the members were lawyers, favoured the judicial process. Certain categories of CPP member should be banned from public office for fifteen years unless they could prove to a specially appointed exemptions commission that they had been forced to join the party against their will, or had opposed it from within.[34] The main principles of these proposals were accepted in the Elections and Public Offices Disqualification Decree of January 1968, but with the difference that the period of disqualification was reduced to ten years, and that certain higher categories of officer in power on the eve of the coup were made ineligible to apply for exemption.[35] After January 1968, wide fluctuations occurred in the NLC policy on disqualification and exemption, mainly due to the failure of decrees to produce the desired results. After five months of outward political calm, the Elections and Public Offices Disqualification (Amendment) (Number 2) Decree was published in June 1968. This increased the categories disqualified to include all former students of the Kwame Nkrumah Ideological Institute, and officers of the 'integral wings' of the CPP down to district level,[36] bringing the total disqualified to over a thousand. The position of January 1968 was restored with a further amendment two months later which reduced the number disqualified to between two and three hundred.[37]

With the onus on those appealing for exemption to demonstrate their innocence, the majority of applicants failed to prove their case. In October 1968, Patrick Quaidoo, the only CPP minister to attack the Nkrumah personality cult after 1960, failed to gain exemption, yet K. A. Gbedemah, one of the CPP's leading organizers until he went into exile in 1961, gained exemption the following month.[38] The *Legon Observer* criticized the exemptions procedure for leaving political questions to a quasi-judicial process,[39] and General Afrifa's reaction to the exemption of Gbedemah was to throw collective responsibility to the wind and demand the repeal of the Disqualification Decree. He now believed that the people must judge who should and who should not hold office.[40] On 11 February 1969, a new Elections and Public Offices Disqualification Decree reduced the number disqualified to 152 named individuals, but with no right to appeal for exemption.[41] The notion of prescribing universally applicable rules to decide who should be disqualified was now replaced by a cruder approach of 'I don't think you are fit to hold office; therefore I won't let you'.

On 28 April 1969, the arbitrary approach of the February decree was combined, in Decree No. 345, with the more comprehensive approach of the 1968 legislation, and without any right of appeal. A variety of categories of people holding public and party office after 1960, down to the level of district commissioner, were disqualified.[42] This decree was published a few weeks after Afrifa, who had earlier opposed any form of disqualification, had taken over the NLC chairmanship. A further amendment came two days later.[43] This only disqualified those holding certain offices on the eve of the coup, and excluded from the ban members of statutory corporations and MPs. Members of the CPP Central Committee, ministers of state, special advisers to the President and regional and district commissioners were still included. The decree of 28 April, which was signed by Afrifa alone, would have disqualified Gbedemah. According to one account, the amendment two days later came after army officers who belonged to Gbedemah's Ewe tribe had threatened to march on the NLC – an indication that disunity in the armed forces was not confined to the highest

levels.[44] Political parties were allowed to function openly
again on 1 May 1969, but competition for power was still not
conducted within clearly defined rules. In June, a decree banned
the People's Popular Party and sixty-eight of its members
from contesting elections. It was alleged that its ultimate aim
was to restore the CPP and Nkrumah to power.[45]

In addition to the possibility of the return of the CPP, 1969
saw the added complication of the attempt by the NLC chairman, General Ankrah, to secure office under civilian rule by
collecting funds from foreign firms and distributing them to
civilian politicians.[48] The immediate result of the discovery of
his action was Ankrah's resignation from the NLC, but the
whole affair served as a reminder that competitors for power
would not necessarily use constitutional or legal means, and
that the NLC therefore had a justification, or an excuse, for
disqualifying some of them in an arbitrary manner.

The whole affair served as a reminder of the extent to which
those who had once been united in their opposition to Dr
Nkrumah, and in their desire to build a better Ghana after his
downfall, were now being drawn into rival camps. The main
contenders in the struggle for power have not yet written their
memoirs, and the full story is not yet clear, but informed
observers were able to put two and two together. The usual
version was that General Ankrah had hopes of becoming
President when civilian rule returned. The type of presidency
envisaged by the Constitutional Commission was a largely
decorative one, with much less power than the President of the
First Republic,[47] but, the story goes, Dr Busia was determined
that if he became Prime Minister he was not going to function
in the shadow of a retired general who had tasted real power,
and was unlikely to be content with nominal power. Once it was
clear that Ankrah would not be allowed to preside over a Busia
government, he sought allies among other politicians not committed to supporting Busia or Gbedemah, the other major con-
tender for the prime ministership. Ankrah was unable to carry
the rest of the NLC with him. General Afrifa's support for

Busia was only very thinly disguised, while Inspector-General Harlley and Commissioner of Police Deku were thought to support Gbedemah, who belonged to the Ewe tribe, as they did. There was now not only a collective desire to make a return of the CPP impossible, but also individual desires on the part of NLC members to secure their own personal careers in the Second Republic. The NLC no longer had the monolothic appearance it had possessed in 1966. Within a few weeks of Ankrah's resignation, his fellow Ga tribesman, Commissioner of Police Nunoo, was forced to resign from the NLC for a breach of official secrecy after becoming publicly involved in a dispute with the Attorney-General, a Busia supporter, over whether Ankrah had given money to four politicians or only one.[48]

The Last Mile

Afrifa succeeded Ankrah as chairman of the NLC, and one of the first actions of his government was to legalize political parties.[49] The Government had already committed itself to restoring civilian rule before the end of the year, and would probably have done so even if General Ankrah had remained in the chair, but the Ankrah affair removed most of the doubts that remained of the wisdom of this course. The NLC had achieved its main objectives and, if it did not bow out at this stage, there was the risk of further splits weakening its cohesion. There remained, however, the question of whether power might be won by a party acting as a front for the CPP.

When the ban on parties was lifted, over ten were formed in May 1969, but only five had survived by August and it was clear that the election would, in practice, be a two-horse race between Dr Kofi Busia's Progress Party, led by men who had opposed Dr Nkrumah, and Komla Gbedemah's National Alliance of Liberals, led by a man who had been one of Nkrumah's senior ministers until he fled the country in 1961, and including in its ranks a greater proportion of former CPP men than any other party. There were no opinion polls to suggest what the result might be, the only pollster having been deported for his part in the Ankrah affair, but the general opinion of Ghanaians who thought they knew the country well was that the result would be close. Gbedemah, they reasoned, had organized successful campaigns in the past, and he had the essential contacts at constituency level. It was not certain that a victory for him would have meant the restoration of the CPP or the arrest of NLC members, and Gbedemah said nothing to suggest that he had such plans, but what was important was that some members of the Government, and many members of the public, did not want to take the risk. The Constituent Assembly, after a heated debate, approved Article 71 of the draft constitution which disqualified from office anyone whose property had been confiscated on the order of a commission of inquiry, due to its unlawful acquisition.[50] This suggested that Gbedemah would be challenged in the courts if elected, but there was still the possibility of the constitution being amended if his party obtained a majority in Parliament. There was still a feeling in some quarters that the NLC was not yet secure.

Less than a fortnight before the general election, the Constituent Assembly hurriedly adopted a proposal that the functions that were originally to have been assigned to a civilian President should be given to a Presidential Commission comprised of the chairman and vice-chairman of the NLC, and the officer commanding the armed forces. The fact that the Assembly had originally rejected the proposal on procedural grounds, and only passed the motion after being asked to reconsider it by the NLC,[51] suggests that a certain amount of pressure was applied by the Government. The NLC was saved from the possible embarrassment of having to amend a constitution that had been approved by a representative body, and now felt it could safely allow the Assembly to enact the constitution, which would have the appearance of a document approved by the people of Ghana rather than by seven uniformed officers.

As far as the Presidential Commission itself was concerned its purpose and value were never entirely clear, but some critics saw it as a potential long-stop that would act as a check on any civilian government that betrayed the ideals for which the NLC had fought. In other words, it might be used to prevent Gbedemah from reviving the CPP.[52] Whether the Commission could have functioned in this way is a matter for speculation. So too is the question of whether the NLC would have handed over power willingly if Gbedemah had won the election. All we do know is that, having got its Commission, the NLC felt sufficiently secure to permit a free election to go ahead as planned on 19 August 1969.

Some supporters of unsuccessful parties questioned the extent to which the election was in fact free. It was a common complaint that Dr Busia's appointment as chairman of the Centre for Civic Education, nearly two years before political parties were legalized, gave him an advantage over his opponents in building up contacts in all the regions, and some candidates reported that many voters were under the impression that the NLC supported Busia. Yet if he gave the impression of being the NLC's 'favourite son', this was largely because the NLC had taken power to remove the CPP, and Busia's anti-CPP credentials appeared stronger than those of any other party leader. While the election, like other contested elections in Ghana, was fought on a variety of local and personal issues, Dr Busia's main appeal to the opinion leaders on whom success depended was to prevent the return of the men who ruled Ghana before 1966. This was an appeal that proved irresistible. The Progress Party won 105 of the 140 seats, and the military men who feared a return of the former regime were able to sleep more easily at night.[53] One of the most important requirements for a military government wanting to hand over power had been met. A successor regime was available which would not threaten the ideals, the freedom or the lives of the uniformed men who had taken power.

Once the election was over, the end of the NLC's road was in sight. Any reader who has travelled widely in Ghana will realize by now that the road back to barracks had much in common with other Ghanaian roads. There were some remarkably smooth stretches, which enabled the travellers to congratulate themselves on how much better things were ordered in Ghana compared with other parts of Africa, but one could never be sure what was lurking round the next corner. There were often unexpected bumps and potholes, and some pessimists wondered whether the destination would ever be reached. Of the eight NLC members who started on the road, one was killed before the halfway stage had been reached, and two others fell by the wayside before the end, but those who survived insisted that there would be no going back. The appointment of the Political Committee in June 1966 was the first major milestone, and the creation of the Constitutional Commission in September that year was the next. The attempted counter-coup in April 1967 threatened to cause a diversion (or worse), but it had the effect of strengthening the determination to reach the end more quickly rather than risking another ambush by delaying. The appointment of civilians to executive positions in central and local government provided further milestones, and the election of the Constituent Assembly in 1968 suggested that the end was not very far away. By August 1969 it was clear that the pessimists were wrong, and in September the travellers arrived with their mission accomplished.

To say that the NLC was able to hand over power relatively easily because the people chose a successor government acceptable to it, leaves us with the question of why the electorate voted in the way they did. The short answer is that Dr Busia was able to obtain the support of the most important opinion leaders in the constituencies, especially the chiefs and prominent businessmen. Their motives for supporting him were varied, and included a calculated gamble in backing the party leader they thought most likely to win, in the expectation of rewards from the Government they had helped to elect. Thus one reason for Busia's victory was the fact that certain key people expected him to win, but this does not explain why they expected him to.

Some observers explained the result in terms of what almost amounted to a 'swing of the pendulum' in Ghanaian politics. Nkrumah had had his chance and had failed, so it was argued. It was now only fair to give an opportunity to those who had been most vigorous in their opposition to him. This view was particularly favoured by Progress Party supporters, both as a means of explaining why people ought to vote for the party, and as an explanation as to why so many did vote for it. Some of the more articulate voters were undoubtedly influenced by the motive of 'giving the other side a chance', but this explanation, like that of 'backing the favourite', does not explain adequately why the Progress Party won such an overwhelming victory. A more convincing argument is that the 1969 election result represented a vote of confidence in the aims behind the *coup d'état* of 1966. Those who were able to deliver this vote were members of the chieftaincy and middle class, who had disliked pre-coup policies which had, they felt, reduced the power and influence of the chieftaincy, narrowed the scope of Ghanaian private enterprise and reduced intellectual freedom. These policies had been largely reversed between 1966 and 1969, and, with political parties illegal for most of that period, the NLC leant heavily on the 'old élite' in order to bridge the gap between government and governed.[54] This group enjoyed a head start when parties were legalized again in May 1969. Dr Nkrumah was in exile, many of his senior colleagues had been disqualified from contesting the election, and Government propaganda over the previous three years had discredited most of his policies. Gbedemah could only rally some of the middle and lower ranks of the old CPP to his side, and many of these people suffered the electoral disadvantage of being branded as comrades of Nkrumah, without the compensating advantage of widespread influence within their local communities. In the circumstances, a party vacuum was filled by the middle class and the chiefs, under the leadership of men who had been prominent in opposing the CPP in the years immediately after independence. Although not many people expected the Progress Party's victory to be as decisive as it in fact was, it now seems that it won in most constituencies because there was no source from which an effective challenge could be mounted against it.

In the early 1960s, one-party rule was seen by many as a 'natural' development in Ghana, as in many other parts of Africa. The ease with which Ghana's single party was toppled in February 1966, and the rapidity with which most traces of support for it sank in the following months, showed the limited foundations on which the party had rested. These appeared to have consisted largely of patronage, bribery, the use of state coercion and a habit of obedience to authority, none of which was any use to the party once it was out of office. The army and police officers were the only sections of the middle class able to undermine the foundations and, having done so, they then turned to other sections of the middle class, and the chiefs, for assistance in advising on, and executing, policy. Because the NLC gave greater power and influence to these groups, their prospects of gaining power, once the military Government had departed, were enhanced. The NLC felt safe to return to barracks and leave power in their hands in 1969, on the assumption that they would not threaten the ideals behind the coup, or the liberty of those who had engineered it.

VIII · Unfinished Business

It would have been pleasant to have concluded this study on the happy note struck at the end of the previous chapter. In August 1969, Ghanaians were able to take part in an activity which is becoming rarer and rarer in African politics – a free election contested by competing parties. A few weeks later, a civilian government was installed, led by a man who had consistently opposed the CPP policies against which the coup had been directed. Three NLC members remained in office as members of the Presidential Commission, until the following August, but they retired from the army and police after taking up their new duty, and their presence did not in any obvious way restrict the civilian Government's freedom of action. Of the remaining members of the military Government, B. A. Yakubu returned to the police force with the rank of inspector-general, and the others retired to comfortable homes in the suburbs of Accra, where they devoted their leisure time to tennis, golf and horse riding. The *coup d'état* of 1966 had succeeded, in the sense that those who had taken power from a group of civilians whose policies they detested, were able to hand it over to another group in whom they had confidence. But the NLC's objectives had always involved something more than a transfer of power from Dr Nkrumah to Dr Busia. There had always been the desire to withdraw from politics in the knowledge that the foundations for a better Ghana had been laid, in terms of both the enjoyment of greater material prosperity and the practice of honest, democratic government. The NLC's contribution to Ghanaian history must be judged largely in terms of the extent to which these foundations had been laid by 1969. This chapter will consider the extent to which the military Government was able to bring about the changes which it felt necessary if democratic government was to be sustained.

A detailed assessment of the NLC's economic performance is outside the scope of this study, but the ability of a community to practice democratic government depends at least partly on the underlying economic conditions. Outside the Communist bloc, it is in the wealthiest countries that democratic political systems flourish most readily, while in the poorest, including most of Africa, Asia and Latin America, governments chosen, or removed, through the medium of the ballot box, are the exception. This may lead to the pessimistic conclusion that any discussion of the prospects of democracy in a country like Ghana is futile. Some students of politics might cross such countries off their list of potential democracies with the firmness of any army medical officer rejecting any potential recruit with flat feet. Others, starting off with the assumption that the prospects for democracy are nil when real income per head is low and static, might expect any advance from this economic base to make some contribution to the emergence of democratic institutions.

The NLC's successes in re-scheduling the country's debts and reducing the balance of payments and budget deficits, were noted in the previous chapter. In raising the national income, its achievements were more limited. In the six years before the coup, a rise of 17·5 per cent in the real gross national product was nearly offset by a 17·1 per cent rise in population.[1] During the period of military rule, the population increased at an estimated average of 2·7 per cent per year, one of the highest rates of increase in Africa,[2] while the real rate of economic growth was only 0·6 per cent in 1966, 1·6 per cent in 1967 and 0·8 per cent in 1968.[3] As 'prestige projects' were scrapped, unemployment rose to new levels. The exact figures are in dispute. At the end of the period of military rule, Dr Busia gave the figure of 600,000 registered unemployed,[4] representing a quarter of the total labour force, but any such figures are suspect in an economy where many of those genuinely unemployed do not register, while some of those who are partially unemployed may do so. Official statistics record only employment, not unemployment. The Central Bureau of Statistics estimated that the total number of workers employed in 1968 was 3,614,000. This was 344,000 less than on the eve of the coup.[5] Whatever the exact figure, it does not require any elaborate economic analysis to demonstrate that unemployment is likely to be high in a country where large cuts are made in public investment at a time when real income per head is virtually static.

It is debatable whether any other government could have accomplished more than the NLC in the economic field, and it is arguable that matters would have been much worse by 1969 but for the change of policy that followed the coup. It may be to the NLC's credit that Ghana did not become still poorer, but such an achievement did not enhance the prospects of democratic government in any positive way. If Ghana did provide more fertile ground for democracy in 1969 than in 1966, the reasons must be sought mainly in the political, rather than the economic changes of the intervening years. Of the features of the political climate at the beginning of the Second Republic which suggested that democracy would fare better than it had in the First, the most important seemed to be the memories that Ghanaians now had of the CPP, the greater willingness to criticize authority, the loss of naïve faith in political leaders, the realization of the inefficiency of personal rule, the greater will to make democracy work, and the realization that the army might intervene again if it did not work.

The Growth of Democratic Ideals

The ideals of freedom and democracy towards which the NLC was striving were considered in Chapter II. The insistence that the Constitution of the Second Republic should make imprisonment without trial and the restoration of a one-party state impossible, reflected the view that, however one defined a democratic political system, one recognized it by certain distinguishing features, including free competition between political parties, freedom of expression, tolerance of criticism and the rule of law.

According to General Ocran:

Democracy means respect for individuality, and other people's views, and tolerance. Consequently, there can be no democracy without certain well-known freedoms such as those of expression, of thought, of person, of assembly and of association. It is therefore inevitable that in every democratic political system there should be an opposition. The opposition should be welcome and embraced. Above all it must not be tribally based or show any ethnic affiliations.[6]

General Afrifa insisted on the need for:

Freedom of worship, of speech and of the press, the right of peaceable assembly, equality before the law, just trial for crime, freedom from unreasonable search, and security from being deprived of life, liberty or property, without due process of law. Herein are the invisible sentinels which guard the door of every home from invasion, coercion, intimidation and fear.[7]

These were the ideals. We can now consider the reasons why they were not realized in the First Republic, and the reasons for believing that they might have become capable of attainment by the advent of the Second.

Writing at a time when Nkrumah was still in power, Bernard Crick contrasted the preservation of free politics in Israel with the emergence of autocracy in Ghana, and suggested that the reason for the difference might have been due to:

the simple fact . . . that in one country there is a greater will to preserve both political freedom and national identity. Perhaps men who have known the deepest and most violent oppression crave for, and become addicted to, personal liberty, while people who have known only insult and injustice may under-value liberty in their desire for national revenge and national prestige.[8]

The phrase 'greater will' suggests that the emergence of dictatorship in Ghana was not simply an inevitable outcome that was to be expected in a country of Ghana's level of development. This view is shared by Dennis Austin:

A leader more careful of individual rights could have led the CPP along more tolerant paths; a longer-established party, having a greater wealth of local talent than the CPP could call on, might have objected to the degree of power which the new republic vested in Nkrumah. An opposition more sensitive of the need to act prudently might have been able to keep open channels of criticism and dissent which, in the event, were choked by the concentration of power first within the single party and then in the hands of the President.[9]

Totalitarian power was alien to them [the CPP] until they felt its authority, and it was then too late to do more than deplore its misuse.[10]

If these views are correct, they suggest that Ghana enjoyed some advantages at the outset of the Second Republic which she did not enjoy at the start of the First. By 1966 the people had experienced a form of government more autocratic than anything they had known under colonial rule, and this made them all the more determined by 1969 that history would not repeat itself. Conditions in Tropical Africa may make dictatorship, like malaria, a greater danger than in many other parts of the world, but those who have suffered from either complaint may take extra care to minimize the possibility of its recurrence.

Apart from the lessons of the First Republic, the period of military rule itself provided a certain amount of training for the democratic era which it was hoped would follow. Attacks on the head of state's views on atheism, or on the pomposity of the motorcades that accompanied him, may not seem important in themselves, but they helped to prevent leaders from being built up into god-like figures. Criticism of policy, as in the case of matters such as the Abbott Agreement and the Golden Triangle road network, became more of a habit, and this habit did not die with the ending of military rule. Another major advantage that Ghana enjoyed by 1969 was a greater realization of the fallibility of political leaders. Much of the praise heaped on Dr Nkrumah when he was President had been made with tongue in cheek by people who realized on which side their bread was buttered, but there were some who genuinely believed that he was endowed with special qualities. The revelations of corruption and incompetence, which were made after his downfall, led many to revise their views.[11]

By deliberately avoiding the personality cult, and by promising to hand over power to civilians as soon as possible, the NLC helped to emphasize that a particular government could be useful for a short period without being indispensable for all time. CPP supporters used to chant 'Nkrumah never dies!' Those who succeeded Nkrumah were more willing to admit that they were mortal, politically. General Ankrah's resignation in April 1969, after he had accepted financial gifts which he had not personally used, helped to emphasize that even heads of state are capable of human errors, and that they may have to give up office as a result. The approach of the 1969 election, like that of elections in many parts of the world, led to the projection of some political leaders as larger than life, but never on the same scale as Nkrumah. One of the side issues of the campaign was the question of whether it was right for Dr Busia's likeness to appear on match boxes or sardine tins, remembering that Ghana had only recently overthrown a man whose head had appeared on the national coinage, and who had erected a statue to himself outside the National Assembly. Dr Busia felt it necessary to defend himself by claiming that the matches and sardines had been intended for sale in Ghana at the time when he was Opposition leader in exile, but that no import licence could be obtained for them before the coup. Projecting an exiled Opposition leader in this way was, apparently, considered less objectionable than using such devices in an election campaign.

One justification for the concentration of power under the CPP had been that, even if it was not always democratic, it was more efficient. By 1969, even ministers who had served under Nkrumah, and who regretted his downfall, were prepared to admit that presidential decisions which by-passed the proper channels did not necessarily contribute to the rapid development that was desired. Civil servants were quick to point out that intelligent democratic discussion might have prevented the waste of £10 million on a massive conference building, or the uneconomic expansion of Ghana Airways. Dictatorship stood condemned by 1969, both because it was unjust and because it was inefficient. Whereas before 1966 politicians were constantly asserting that a competitive party system would be alien to Ghana, and that 'democratic centralism' (with the emphasis, in practice, on the centralism) met the country's needs more adequately, by 1969 any centralists who remained were drowned by the chorus that demanded a constitution with elaborate checks and balances, in order to safeguard individual liberty. Despite the amendment of some of the proposals of the Constitutional Commission which it thought would make for inflexibility, the Constituent Assembly accepted the spirit of the proposals, and most of the safeguards remained intact. The powers of the Prime Minister were to be restricted by the presence of a President and a Council of State, the enactments of Parliament were to be challengeable in the courts, and certain entrenched clauses were to be incapable of amendment. The prevention of tyranny was now seen as an objective at least as important as the achievement of rapid economic growth.

If ability to contrast the country's experiences before and after 24 February 1966 gave many Ghanaians a greater desire to seek a democratic political system, the manner in which the change of government was brought about on that date also taught them certain lessons. The army and police showed one way in which politicians who strayed from the democratic path

could be dealt with, and there was every reason to believe that
they would intervene again if a future government behaved
in the same way as Nkrumah's. Here was a check on the power
of the executive that might prove as effective as any contained
in the 1969 Constitution. In 1964, W. F. Gutteridge was not
alone in believing that military regimes were unlikely in
Africa.[12] At a conference on Africa's élite classes held at
Ibadan University in the same year, P. C. Lloyd felt able to
declare that 'in few of the independent states is the military
élite much in evidence in the social and political life'.[13] Most
CPP leaders would probably have agreed. Since 1964, the ease
with which the military have taken and retaken power in
many African states provides a warning to any politician with
a Messiah complex. While General Kotoka's reaction to a
question on what he would do if the people elected a government similar to the CPP was one of utter disbelief that they
would ever do such a thing, General Ocran was more forthcoming. He could not go back to a military career and remain
'politically indifferent'.[14] In his book, he adopted a more
detached view:

> Will the military ever take up arms again? Your guess is as
> good as mine. However, the answer depends very much on
> the showing of the next civilian government. In the final
> analysis it is the future government's performance that will
> either keep the soldiers in barracks or bring them out again,
> rifle in hand, to seize power.[15]

Commissioner of Police Yakubu was another NLC member
who felt it necessary to stress that the transfer of power to
civilians would be conditional. He would continue his career as
a policeman after military rule ended, but he 'would not stand
for' the return of one-party rule and arbitrary arrests.[16]

The main hopes for democracy, then, rested on two assumptions: that the people's experience of tyranny in the First
Republic would make them less gullible in putting their trust in
politicians, and that if politicians took more power into their

own hands in spite of this, then the army might intervene. A greater desire to create and operate democratic institutions might be buttressed by the threat to depose by force those who flouted the spirit of the constitution.

Can Democracy Take Root?

The enthusiasm with which Ghanaians celebrated the 1969 election results and the return to civilian rule was infectious. In Kumasi, which had been a major centre of opposition to Dr Nkrumah, the 'Victory Day' atmosphere was unmistakable. Other towns were more restrained, but the feeling, especially among the educated minority, that a new chapter in Ghanaian history was opening, was difficult to escape. The features of Ghanaian politics that had changed during the previous three and a half years were obvious, but it was possible that the unchanging features might prove the important ones, once the victory celebrations were over. The NLC had tried to enable democracy to flower anew, but was the soil in which this plant was rooted radically different from the soil in which the CPP had flourished before 1966? If it was not, would the desire to nurture the tender plant of democracy not prove in vain? The army might forcibly uproot the plant, if politicians perverted its shape, but the army's value lies in its ability to destroy tyranny, rather than in its ability to create or sustain democracy. Of the features of Ghanaian politics which had changed little, if at all, since 1966, there were three which seemed capable of threatening the survival of democracy: the type of issues on which Ghanaian political battles are usually fought; the advantages of supporting the winning side, and the corresponding difficulties in building an effective opposition; and the lack of experience in practising democratic politics.

The issues around which Ghanaian politics revolve can be classified into four overlapping groups: personality, national security, economic and constitutional. Taking the NLC period as an example, the thirteen most important issues could be classified thus:

Issue:	Person-ality	Security	Economic	Constitu-tional
Disqualification from Public Office:	×	×	—	×
Agreements with foreign firms:	×	—	×	—
Protection of Ghanaian enterprise:	×	—	×	—
Public appointments:	×	—	—	—
Treatment of CPP members (including Protective Custody):	×	×	—	×
Relations with Communist Countries:	—	×	—	—
Cocoa price:	—	—	×	—
Priorities in imports:	×	—	×	—
Foreign debts:	—	—	×	—
Labour relations (especially strikes):	—	×	×	—
Civilian rule programme:	×	—	—	×
De-centralization:	—	—	—	×
Chieftaincy disputes:	×	—	—	—

The list suggests that ten of the thirteen types of problem with which the NLC had to deal involved personalities or security. The distinctive feature of the security issues was that they required decisions on which the survival of the Government, and the personal safety of its members, depended. The personality issues were those that had to be resolved by taking decisions which might be interpreted as being designed to benefit or harm a particular individual, or a small group of easily identifiable individuals. Any debate on the civilian rule programme, or the scope of disqualification from office, could not be conducted without the realization that the final decision would affect the individual careers of Busia and Gbedemah. A decision on whether to make reflective number plates on cars compulsory might imply deciding whether or not to enrich the owner of the only firm producing or distributing them, and decisions on import licences frequently had similar implications.

While some of the issues of the NLC period, such as disqualification and the civilian rule programme, arose because of the nature of military rule, many have been common to Ghanaian politics for as long as Ghanaians have been running their own affairs. There are three main reasons for this. Firstly, the smallness of the country's population frequently gives rise to situations in which the clients with whom men in power have to deal are personal acquaintances, and not merely representatives of impersonal pressure groups. Secondly, the level of economic development is such that decisions may have to be taken in particular, rather than general, terms. A decision on the allocation of licences for the importation of biscuits may involve ruling not whether licences should go to firms employing over a hundred workers, but whether Mr X's firm should be given a licence. Thirdly, all Ghanaian governments have chosen to follow policies that involve economic intervention, with the result that people have come to expect matters affecting their daily lives, on issues ranging from whether their villages should have piped water to whether their firms should be given more contracts, to be settled by the Government rather than by the forces of supply and demand. A government that wants to turn its back on nepotism, bribery and corruption, may attempt to take decisions on the basis of factors other than whether an applicant for an import licence is the cousin of a minister, or whether a village demanding piped water voted for the ruling party. It was argued in Chapter VI that the NLC did introduce a greater rationality into decision-making, but the process of policy-making must always depend to some extent on the nature of the raw material of public demands that are being processed. Democracy may flourish relatively easily where the subjects of public debate are general ('Reduce direct taxation!'; 'Make the schools comprehensive!'; 'Increase the scope of the health service!'). Where they are particular ('Give my firm an import licence!'; 'Give our town a secondary school!'; 'Locate the new hospital in my constituency!'), there is the danger that democratic discussion on priorities may degenerate into a series of personal, local and tribal squabbles.

Whether political debates on the general merits of comprehensive education are morally superior to debates on which towns should be given new schools is a matter of opinion, but one of the consequences of the latter type of debate becoming predominant is that the scope for a Parliamentary dialogue between government and opposition, which the 1969 Constitution assumed would sustain democracy, is reduced. If there are no significant differences between the political parties on matters of principle, policy or priority, and it was difficult to detect any before or after the 1969 election, beyond the 'more anti-CPP than thou' speeches of some candidates, then it is difficult for the Opposition to attract the support it needs in order to pose as a serious alternative government. Constitution makers may assert that a strong opposition is essential for democracy, and perhaps they are right, but for the man in the bush, and still more for the man in business, the sensible course is to follow the party that wields power, in the hope that it will use some of that power for his benefit. At worst, this can lead to a cynical 'If you can't beat them, bribe them' attitude. At best, it may lead to a benevolent form of one-party rule, once it becomes clear how little will be achieved by supporting opposition parties.

Inspector-General Harlley's observation, made over two years before the end of military rule, that a democratic constitution would not alone guarantee democracy[17] seemed to lose none of its validity after the return of civilian rule. An early test of the effectiveness of the 1969 constitution came early in 1970, when Dr Busia's Government dismissed 568 public servants. One of these, E. K. Sallah, challenged the Government's right to dismiss him, and the Supreme Court ruled in his favour. Dr Busia responded by rejecting the court's competence. He insisted that 'No court can enforce any decision that seeks to compel the Government to employ or re-employ anyone'.[18]

If the Prime Minister's reaction was disturbing to those who had hoped that the judiciary would be able to check the power of the executive, the messages of support he received were equally disturbing for those who had hoped that sycophants had been replaced by citizens with a more mature political judgement. Some of these messages were printed in the Progress Party's official newspaper:

> The greatness of your wisdom and faith and respect for the rule of law and the sincere toleration of the Progress Party government in upholding the principles of democracy to stay and maintain Ghana is clearly and sufficiently demonstrated.
> (Newspaper's lack of punctuation.)

> Under your able and polished leadership, justice is an eternal value and universal in the human heart and does not matter who dispenses it efficiently and impartially.
> (*sic*)

> Congratulations for your bold speech, more grease to your elbow, God bless you.

> Don't relax or else the enemies will capture us.

> Until your broadcast last Monday night, I was the most unhappy man in Ghana. Today, I am the proudest, it was a wonderful performance.

> Congratulations on your bold and beautiful speech last Monday night.[19]

At the outset of the Second Republic, unlike the latter years of the First, politicians of all parties accepted, in principle, such ideals as the separation of powers, the rule of law and a competitive party system, but for all the volume of speeches, books and pamphlets on the virtues of liberal democracy, they had had very little experience in operating it. Nkrumah had been able to adapt a Westminster-type constitution to purposes that would never have been tolerated at Westminster, with the people unable or unwilling to stop him. The NLC, for all its tolerance, had been able to resort to arbitrary power in the last extreme. Why, then, should a new civilian government

F

(or a civilian opposition) suddenly start showing respect for the principles of a democratic constitution if these conflicted with what it wanted to do? One answer might be the one suggested earlier in this chapter – that memories of the CPP Government might remind politicians of what ultimately happened to those who took excessive power into their own hands, and that similar memories might make the governed less docile. The possibilities are not, however, confined to the Westminster model and the CPP model. It is conceivable that something closer to the Colonial Office model might emerge. The country could be ruled by educated, well-meaning men who do not automatically brand their critics as heretics, or bundle them into gaol; who are flexible enough to meet some public criticism, but who may effectively block the paths of politicians who threaten to take power from them. The model could not, of course, be followed rigidly, because the colonial rulers eventually accepted that they had to surrender power, but for many years they provided Ghana with a form of benevolent oligarchy, less harsh in its method of ruling than the CPP, and this form of government may come more naturally to Ghanaians than the democratic ideal which the NLC, the Constitutional Commission, and the Constituent Assembly, apparently wanted.

In politics, as in economics, the military Government left a legacy of unfinished business. In both, it was more successful in destroying what it disliked than in building what it desired. It was easier to reduce the balance of payments and budget deficits than to carry out a successful programme of rural development, and it was easier to destroy the CPP than to build a democratic state in its place. NLC members made it clear that their ideal was a democratic form of government, operating under the rule of law, as the remarks of Afrifa and Ocran, quoted earlier in this chapter, show. These were hopes for the future, but they could be no more than hopes. General Ocran's remarks about the need for a strong, non-ethnic opposition had a particularly ironic ring after the 1969 election, which produced an opposition which was numerically weak (29 out of 140 MPs), and ethnically based (18 out of its 29 seats were won in predominently Ewe constituencies in the Volta and Eastern regions). As for General Afrifa's faith in the rule of law, the first major clash between the new civilian Government and the judiciary, over the Sallah case, suggested the practical limits to the effectiveness of judicial influence.

If the military had not staged their coup in 1966, many of the features that characterized Ghanaian politics by 1969 would never have emerged. Supporters of the NLC could point out that there would have been no free election, no pressure groups openly articulating their demands and no newspapers expressing controversial opinions. Hundreds of men might still have been in prison without trial, with thousands of others fearing the same fate, and intelligent men might still have been pretending to proclaim their faith in the philosophy of Nkrumaism instead of debating the issues of the real world around them. The NLC's achievement was that it had demolished the CPP edifice, and had allowed the people to set up a free market in political ideas and political demands on the site where the edifice once stood. Soldiers and policemen could suggest the sort of permanent buildings they would like to see constructed on the site, including a 'loyal opposition' and an independent judiciary, but the final layout, and the way in which it was used, depended on civilians. The NLC could not itself produce a loyal opposition to provide a check on the Government in the years to come, and, short of using armed force again, it could not deal with politicians who ignored the rulings of the judiciary. In the long run, the course of Ghanaian political history may depend on the extent to which the lessons the country had learnt by 1969 have given people the will to ensure that the democrat triumphs, on a political and social terrain that still gives many tactical advantages to the autocrat. People cannot be forced to be free, not even by soldiers and policemen.

IX · Conclusion

We have traced the life of the military Government from start to finish. Its birth was comparatively painless, but when it came into the world it possessed few qualifications for the station into which it had been born, beyond the basic one of self defence. To function adequately, it required, and received, the assistance of a variety of civilians who possessed many of the qualities that it lacked. As it grew to maturity, it became more capable of planning its own future and, after realizing most of its ambitions, it decided to retire at an early age. The legacy it left behind included a sounder economy than the one it had inherited, and a democratic constitution, but it could not guarantee that its successors would not squander these assets.

The story of the NLC is a success story, in the sense that it attained its most important objectives. It failed to achieve any real economic growth, or to reduce the level of unemployment, but in the circumstances these tasks would probably have been beyond the capacity of most civilian governments. One major achievement was to transform a one-party state, in which any form of open political competition had been stifled, into a state in which political competition and free expression were once again permitted. The other was to arrest the worsening economic conditions in which budget deficits, balance of payments deficits and foreign debts had been increasing. The successes were due to two main factors; the qualities of the NLC itself, and the reponse to the actions of the NLC of many sections of the community which it was governing.

One of the most valuable qualities of the NLC was the modesty of its members. If they had started by announcing plans for raising the standard of living rapidly, for clearing all the urban slums, or for providing secondary education for all, future historians would almost certainly have had to write them off as a failure. Instead, they set themselves the more modest, but still formidable, targets of economic stability and the restoration of democratic government. Their modesty was revealed again by their willingness to be guided by the advice of others, and by their willingness to delegate much of the business of government to civilians. In Chapters II, III, IV and V we saw the large part that pressure groups, civil servants and civilian commissioners were able to play in influencing and executing policy. Finally, the NLC's modesty was important in ensuring that it did not outstay its welcome. If it had stayed in power for an extra year or two it is possible that internal dissension would have weakened the Government, and that continued austerity, without the compensation of political freedom, would have led to widespread public discontent. As it was, the NLC stayed in power long enough to acquire some of the virtues of politicians, without acquiring too many of the vices. Of the virtues, one of the most important was the ability to distinguish between objectives which were fundamental, because they were related to the NLC's survival or to its whole *raison d'être*, such as the civilian rule programme, disqualification from office, or internal security; and those policies which were not directly related to the presence of a military government, such as the re-negotiation of foreign debts or the making of agreements with foreign firms. The NLC left the pursuit of the latter policies largely in the hands of civilian commissioners and civil servants, thus leaving itself free to concentrate on the relatively small range of issues which affected the survival and duration of the military Government, or which were closely related to the basic ideals behind the coup. The political vices acquired by the NLC appear to have been relatively few. Some purists complained that, in the later years, decisions on matters such as the allocation of contracts were sometimes influenced by the desire to please men who might become influential political figures after the return of civilian rule, and the Ankrah affair suggests that at least one NLC member tried to insure his political future before parties had been legalized, but there was never corruption or patronage on a scale comparable with that of the First Republic.

Much of the literature on military government places the emphasis on the backgrounds and qualities of the military men themselves, often with the assumption that people with army backgrounds tend to bring with them a distinctive bundle of acquired values and administrative techniques when they enter politics.

> The army differs in function from the society that surrounds it and its function requires that it be separate and segregated. It requires a common uniform, and this immediately distinguishes it from the civilian masses. It requires separate housing, in purely military quarters, the barracks. It demands a systematised nomadism moving from one garrison town to another. It demands a separate code of morals and manners from that of the civilian population . . . . All this tends to enhance military solidarity by making the military life self-centred. It is easy, even, to inspire contempt for one's own nationals – the 'civvies' . . . .[1]

> The strictly hierarchical arrangement calls for the issue of exceptionally straightforward instructions from superior to subordinate, and the nature of the situation may require a greater latitude of discretion than these allow for. Similarly there may be a tendency to underrate the importance of consultation and thereby gradually to encourage the isolation of the leadership from the lower levels of society. This is in any case encouraged as between the defence forces, other than the police, and the people by the segregated military way of life which the British and the French have passed on to their former colonies.[2]

> Politics to them [the NLC] was indeed the giving of correct orders.[3]

Such notions of soldier-politicians having a different approach to government from civilian politicians can be supported by giving examples of the actions and words of military men in power. In the case of Ghana, General Kotoka's remarks about 'satisfying the people's needs' having a greater meaning to him than socialism, or General Ankrah's lecture to erring civil servants on the virtues of punctuality, might be quoted as examples of the soldierly approach. The fact that a man has spent most of his career in the army or police will, undoubtedly, have the effect of moulding his character in certain ways, and this may affect his style if he becomes directly involved in an executive capacity in national political activity, but the same is true of lawyers, businessmen or carpenters who enter politics. With experience, however, those who stay in politics long enough usually acquire some of the necessary skills, whatever their original backgrounds. The study of Ghana between 1966 and 1969 suggests that NLC members were, basically, inexperienced politicians, who enjoyed certain advantages and suffered certain handicaps as a result of having taken power suddenly, and by force. Some of them showed a certain political naïvety in the early months, but this was due as much to inexperience in governing as to the nature of their previous occupations. It would be going too far to assert that NLC members were simply members of the middle class in khaki suits, but their outlook and their approach to politics had much in common with the rest of the middle class. Sandhurst, the Metropolitan Police Training College and the officers' mess had some influence on them, but so too did experiences and values shared with middle-class civilians. These included education at mission schools, and resentment at the way in which men regarded as social and educational inferiors had wielded power under Dr Nkrumah, and at the consequences of CPP policies.

The fact that power had been taken through the use of armed force obviously had some effect on the way in which the Government organized its affairs, and issues such as disqualification and the preparations for a successor regime, arose largely because of the military/police nature of the Government, but on most political issues, it is useful to regard the NLC as part of a larger social class rather than merely as the head of two groups of uniformed men. The NLC was able to achieve its main objectives largely because it concentrated, as a collective body, on a relatively small number of tasks which were within its capacity, while leaving many other functions to civilians in whom it had confidence. While the vast majority of Ghanaians, like the majority of people in most African states, wielded no political influence in their own right, there was a significant minority which did have the power either to provide the NLC with the expertise it required, or to make its task almost impossible. This minority included the chiefs, and some of the thirty to forty thousand people with secondary education. Once the co-operation of this minority had been obtained, there was little to fear from the remaining eight million inhabitants, most of whom were too inarticulate to do more than follow the lead given by the chiefs and the middle class. Within the latter two groups were people with a variety of talents, who were able and willing to take many burdens from the shoulders of the NLC, and people who were able to provide a successor regime which would neither threaten to destroy what the NLC had built, nor threaten the lives and liberty of NLC members.

The quality of civilian talent was a great asset to the NLC. Within a few days of the coup it was able to assemble an Economic Committee composed of two graduates each from London, Durham and Harvard, and one from Cambridge.[4] Later, it was able to appoint civilian commissioners from among the ranks of men with business, administrative and professional qualifications, and to find politicians and lawyers to guide it on the path of civilian rule. Outside the Government and the bodies that advised it, leaders of many influential sections of the community, including chiefs, businessmen and academics, made life easier for the Government by providing their co-operation. The willingness of so many educated and influential civilians to co-operate was due largely to their support for the ideals which had motivated the coup. While the army and police had had their own quarrels with Dr Nkrumah's Government, these were a microcosm of a wider range of grievances. Dislike of what were regarded as the mis-spending of public money, of the neglect of necessities, of political interference in many aspects of daily life, and of the loss of personal freedom, were feelings shared by uniformed men and civilians alike. The uniformed men had the guns, and they were able to do what many civilians would have done themselves, if they had had the opportunity. The description of NLC members as 'liberators of the nation' was not merely a slogan used to give respectability to a group of adventurers, but a reflection of what leaders of many sections of the community felt. The feeling that civilians had a debt to the NLC was important in explaining their willingness to co-operate, and in explaining the relative smoothness with which the Government operated between 1966 and 1969.

The Government was a military/police one throughout, in the sense that the NLC possessed a monopoly of legislative power and control over patronage, so that it could always stifle any political initiative it disliked, but the Government's achievements stem largely from the fact that it was able to leave many functions in the hands of trusted civilians who shared its basic ideals. Once it was convinced that civilians of this type were capable of attracting enough mass support to form an elected government, to the exclusion of the type of civilians who had been forced out of office in 1966, the NLC's work was done. The coup, and the period of military rule that followed, had achieved their objective. In September 1969, satisfied that it had fulfilled its self-imposed task, Ghana's army marched back to barracks.

Notes

CHAPTER I

1. See especially A. A. Afrifa, *The Ghana Coup*, London, Frank Cass, 1966; D. G. Austin, *Politics in Ghana*, London, Oxford University Press, 1964; P. Barker, *Operation Cold Chop*, Accra, Ghana Publishing Corporation, 1969; G. Bing, *Reap the Whirlwind*, London, McGibbon and Kee, 1968; B. Fitch and M. Oppenheimer, *Ghana: The End of an Illusion*, New York, Monthly Review Press, 1966; H. Bretton, *The Rise and Fall of Kwame Nkrumah*, London, Pall Mall Press, 1966; K. Nkrumah, *Dark Days in Ghana*, London, Lawrence and Wishart, 1968; A. K. Ocran, *A Myth is Broken*, Harlow, Longmans, 1969; T. P. Omari, *Kwame Nkrumah: the Anatomy of an African Dictatorship*, Accra, Moxon Paperbacks, 1970.
2. *Daily Graphic*, Accra, 25 February 1966.
3. A. A. Afrifa, *op. cit.*, p. 102.
4. A. K. Ocran, *op. cit.*, pp. 28–39.
5. *ibid.*, p. 43.
6. *ibid.*, p. 44.
7. *ibid.*, p. 43. This is probably an exaggeration. Central Bureau of Statistics figures show that prices only doubled over the period 1952–65. *Economic Survey*, Ghana Publishing Corporation, 1965, p. 147.
8. *Daily Graphic*, 28 February 1966.
9. *ibid.*, 3 March 1966.
10. S. P. Huntington, *Political Order in Changing Societies*, Yale, Yale University Press, 1968, p. 221.

CHAPTER II

1. K. Nkrumah, *Dark Days in Ghana*, London, Lawrence and Wishart, 1968, p. 30.
2. *Daily Graphic*, 25 February to 3 March 1966.
3. *ibid.*, 17 March 1966.

4. *ibid.*, 7 March 1966.
5. *The Man on Horseback*, London, Pall Mall Press, 1962, Chapter 7.
6. *Daily Graphic*, 25 February 1966.
7. *ibid.*, 2 March 1966.
8. NLC *Decree* 1, 26 February 1966.
9. *Daily Graphic*, 28 February 1966.
10. For the text of the broadcasts, see K. Nkrumah, *Voice from Conakry*, London, Panaf Publications, 1967.
11. *Daily Graphic*, 2 May 1966.
12. *ibid.*, 29 April 1966.
13. *ibid.*, 24 March 1966.
14. *ibid.*, 25 March 1966.
15. *ibid.*, 3 March 1966.
16. *ibid.*, 9 April 1966.
17. See Chapter VII.
18. See especially the *Reports* of the Apaloo Commission on Kwame Nkrumah's Properties (1966); the Ollennu Commission on Irregularities in the Granting of Import Licences (1967), and the Jiagge, Manyo-Plange and Sowah Commissions on the Assets of Specified Persons (1968 and 1969) all issued by the Ghana Publishing Corporation.
19. *1960 Population Census*, Vol. III, Ghana Publishing Corporation, 1960, p. 28.
20. See especially Trades Union Congress, *Memorandum on some Measures Aimed at Reducing Prices and the Cost of Living*, Ghana Publishing Corporation, 1966.
21. NLC *Decree* 299, 5 November 1968.
22. *Reap the Whirlwind*, London, McGibbon and Kee, 1968, Chapter 8.
23. *Towards Nkrumaism*, Accra, TUC, 1962, pp. 45–7.
24. *Daily Graphic*, 13 January 1965.
25. *ibid.*, 9 February 1965.
26. *ibid.*, 3 March 1965.
27. 'Parliament in Republican Ghana', *Parliamentary Affairs*, Vol. XVI, No. 4, 1963, p. 386.
28. *Modernisation in Ghana and the USSR*, London, Routledge and Kegan Paul, 1969, p. 100.
29. K. Nkrumah, *op. cit.*, pp. 64–5.
30. *Reap the Whirlwind*, p. 290.
31. Ghana Parliamentary *Debates*, 5 October 1962.
32. *Daily Graphic*, 16 June 1965.

33. *ibid.*, 8 April 1965.
34. See especially the Busia *Report* on University Institutions, Accra, Ghana Publishing Corporation, 1967.
35. *Legon Observer*, University of Ghana, Legon, 28 October 1966.
36. *Reap the Whirlwind*, p. 408.
37. *Daily Graphic*, 11 March 1966.
38. Ghana Parliamentary *Debates*, 22 February 1966.
39. *Daily Graphic*, 15 March 1966.
40. *ibid.*, 26 March 1966.
41. *ibid.*, 27 March 1967.
42. *ibid.*, 2 December 1967.
43. *Legon Observer*, 17 February 1967.
44. *West Africa*, London, 26 October 1968, p. 1270.
45. *Reap the Whirlwind*, p. 449.
46. K. Nkrumah, *op. cit.*, p. 73.
47. Ministry of Information, *A New Era in Ghana*, Accra, Ghana Publishing Corporation, 1966, p. 11.
48. NLC *Decree* 26, 24 March 1966.
49. NLC *Decree* 229, 23 February 1968; *Government Gazette*, July 1968.
50. *A New Era in Ghana*, p. 21.
51. NLC *Decree* 59, 24 June 1966.
52. NLC *Decree* 188, 21 July 1967.
53. *Daily Graphic*, 25 and 27 July 1966.
54. *ibid.*, 12 March 1966.
55. *Report* of the Educational Review Committee, Accra, Ghana Publishing Corporation, 1967.
56. de Graft Johnson *Report*, Accra, State Publishing Corporation, 1966.
57. See especially E. Y. Twumasi, 'Ghana's Draft Constitutional Proposals', *Transition*, October 1968.
58. J. J. Johnson (ed.), *The Role of the Military in Underdeveloped Countries*, Princeton, N.J., Princeton University Press, 1962, p. 54.
59. *ibid.*, p. 247.
60. *Reap the Whirlwind*, p. 415.
61. K. Nkrumah, *op. cit.*, p. 74.
62. A. A. Afrifa, *The Ghana Coup*, London, Frank Cass, 1966.
63. For biographies see Ministry of Information, *The Rebirth of Ghana*, Accra, State Publishing Corporation, 1966, pp. 6–20. For an extreme view of the influence of British values on NLC

policy, see R. M. Price, 'A Theoretical Approach to Military Rule in New States: Reference Group Theory and the Ghanaian Case', *World Politics*, April 1971.

64. A. A. Afrifa, *op. cit.*, p. 111.
65. *Daily Graphic*, 1 March 1966.
66. *ibid.*, 16 August 1966.
67. See T. Hodgkin, *African Political Parties*, Harmondsworth, Penguin, 1961.
68. See especially B. Fitch and M. Oppenheimer, *Ghana: The End of an Illusion*, New York, Monthly Review Press, 1966, Chapter 5; G. Bing, *Reap the Whirlwind*, Chapter 8.
69. *Daily Graphic*, 12 March 1966.
70. *ibid.*, 6 January 1967.
71. *ibid.*, 19 March 1966.
72. *ibid.*, 26 March 1966.
73. *ibid.*, 28 March 1966.
74. *ibid.*, 6 July 1966.
75. *ibid.*, 29 July 1966.
76. *ibid.*, 24 January 1967.
77. *ibid.*, 28 April 1967.
78. *ibid.*, 29 June 1968.
79. *ibid.*, 9 May 1966.
80. *ibid.*, 11 May 1966.
81. NLC *Decree* 112, 2 December 1966.
82. NLC *Decree* 203.
83. *Daily Graphic*, 6 December 1966.
84. *ibid.*, 2 April 1966.
85. *ibid.*, 20 May 1966.
86. *ibid.*, 25 January 1966.
87. *ibid.*, 16 August 1966.
88. *West Africa*, 2 November 1968, p. 1298.
89. NLC *Decree* 49, 24 May 1966; *Daily Graphic*, 6 June 1966.
90. *West Africa*, 3 May 1969, p. 511.
91. *ibid.*, 23 November 1968, p. 1385.
92. *ibid.*, 21 December 1968, p. 1523.
93. *ibid.*, 29 March 1969, p. 366.
94. *Daily Graphic*, 3 March 1966.
95. *ibid.*, 24 June 1966.
96. NLC *Decree* 207, 19 September 1967.
97. *Daily Graphic*, 11 May 1967.
98. *ibid.*, 19 May 1967.

99. *ibid.*, 15 March 1967.

100. *ibid.*, 14 October 1967.

101. *ibid.*, 28 July 1968.

102. *Government Policy on the Promotion of Ghanaian Business Enterprises*, Accra, Ghana Publishing Corporation, 1968.

103. *White Paper*, 3/67, Accra, Ghana Publishing Corporation, 1967.

104. *White Paper*, 11/68, on the Blay Report, Ministry of Information, 1968.

105. *Daily Graphic*, 5 August 1967.

106. *ibid.*, 18 September 1967.

107. *ibid.*, 6 November 1967.

108. *White Paper* on Government Promotion of Ghanaian Business Enterprises, 1968.

109. NLC *Decree* 259, 12 July 1968.

110. *West Africa*, 18 January 1969, p. 72.

111. *Sunday Mirror*, Accra, 5 June 1966.

112. *Daily Graphic*, 25 August 1966.

113. *ibid.*, 16 August 1966.

114. *ibid.*, 27 September 1966.

115. *ibid.*, 17 April 1967.

116. *ibid.*, 23 June 1967.

117. *ibid.*, 19 April 1968.

118. *ibid.*, 19 September 1967.

119. *ibid.*, 21 September 1967.

120. *ibid.*, 23 September 1967.

121. *ibid.*, 14 November 1967.

122. *ibid.*, 3 December 1967.

123. *West Africa*, 30 November 1968, p. 1416.

124. *Legon Observer*, 17 February 1967.

125. *ibid.*, 22 December 1967.

126. *Daily Graphic*, 4 July 1966.

127. *ibid.*, 1 April 1967.

128. See Industrial Relations Act, 1958.

129. *Daily Graphic*, 12 December 1966.

130. *ibid.*, 20 December 1966.

131. See Dr Busia's speech to the TUC, 31 July 1970, reported in *Ghanaian Times*, 3 August 1970.

132. *Daily Graphic*, 1 January 1968.

133. *ibid.*, 27 May 1968.

134. *West Africa*, 3 May 1969, p. 510.

CHAPTER III

1. *Daily Graphic*, 5 June 1967.
2. *ibid.*, 18 April 1967; 10 May 1967.
3. *West Africa*, 30 November 1968, p. 1423.
4. *ibid.*, 28 December 1968, p. 1551.
5. *ibid.*, 14 September 1968, p. 1082.
6. *Dark Days in Ghana*, London, Lawrence and Wishart, 1968, p. 28.
7. *Daily Graphic*, 7 December 1967.
8. NLC *Decree* 161, 22 April 1967; 164, 16 May 1967; 167, 18 May 1967; 172, 24 May 1967; 179, 14 June 1967.
9. NLC *Decree* 131, 28 January 1967.
10. NLC *Decree* 93, 4 October 1966.
11. See especially Harlley's interview with the *Legon Observer*, 19 July 1968.
12. *Daily Graphic*, 6 May 1967.
13. *ibid.*, 23 January 1967.
14. *ibid.*, 17 February 1967.
15. *Legon Observer*, 17 February 1967.
16. *ibid.*
17. *Daily Graphic*, 17 April 1967.
18. *ibid.*, 13 October 1966 and 3 June 1967.
19. *Legon Observer*, 17 February 1967.
20. *Daily Graphic*, 14 July 1966; *West Africa*, 14 September 1968, p. 1082; and *Legon Observer*, 20 January 1967.
21. *Daily Graphic*, 22 March 1967.
22. *Legon Observer*, 31 March 1967.
23. *Daily Graphic*, 1 September 1966.
24. *ibid.*, 14 March 1966.
25. *ibid.*, 27 May 1967.
26. *ibid.*, 29 and 31 May and 1 June, 1967.
27. *ibid.*, 19 April 1966; *Sunday Mirror* (Accra), 24 April 1966.
28. *Legon Observer*, 2 August 1968.
29. *Daily Graphic*, 11 May 1966.
30. *ibid.*, 28 March 1967.
31. *ibid.*
32. *Legon Observer*, 19 August 1966.
33. *ibid.*, 30 September 1966.
34. *Legon Observer*, 14 October 1966. See NLC *Decrees*, 92, 93.
35. *Legon Observer*, 6 December 1968, 28 February 1969.
36. NLC *Decree*, 3, 28 February 1966.

37. *Daily Graphic*, 1 February 1967 and 19 August 1967; and *West Africa*, 8 February 1969, p. 163.
38. *Legon Observer*, 17 February 1967.
39. *ibid.*
40. *Daily Graphic*, 27 May 1967.
41. *ibid.*, 3 June 1967.
42. *ibid.*, 21 February 1967.
43. *Legon Observer*, 15 September 1967.
44. *ibid.*, 8 December 1967.
45. *Daily Graphic*, 15 January 1968.
46. A. K. Armah, *The Beautyful Ones are not yet Born*, London, Heinemann, 1969, p. 184.
47. Pp. 33–44.

CHAPTER IV

1. *Sunday Mirror*, Accra, 27 February 1966.
2. *Daily Graphic*, 21 March 1966.
3. NLC *Decree* 11, 12 March 1966.
4. Ministry of Information, *A New Era in Ghana*, Accra, State Publishing Corporation, 1966, pp. 21–3.
5. *Legon Observer*, 17 February 1967.
6. For a detailed discussion of the incompatibility of some NLC aims, see Chapter V.
7. *Reap the Whirlwind*, London, McGibbon and Kee, 1968, p. 37.
8. D. G. Austin, *Politics in Ghana 1946–60*, London, Oxford University Press, 1964, pp. 411–12.
9. *Reap the Whirlwind*, p. 398.
10. *Daily Graphic*, 1 January 1968.
11. *ibid.*, 24 and 28 June 1966.
12. *ibid.*, 28 June 1966.
13. *ibid.*, 1 July 1967.
14. K. Nkrumah, *Dark Days in Ghana*, London, Lawrence and Wishart, 1968, p. 47.
15. *Daily Graphic*, 25 August 1966.
16. *ibid.*, 17 May 1968.
17. *Budget Statement, 1968–9*, Accra, Ghana Publishing Corporation, 1969.
18. NLC Economic Committee, *Ghana's Economy and Aid Requirements*, Accra, Ghana Publishing Corporation, 1967, p. 16.

19. Armah *v.* Government of Ghana, *All England Law Report*, 4 October 1966, pp. 196–7.
20. See Chapter VII.
21. *Legon Observer*, 31 March 1967.
22. *ibid.*, 17 February 1967.
23. A. K. Ocran, *A Myth is Broken*, Harlow, Longmans, 1969, p. 94.
24. *Legon Observer*, 8 July 1966.
25. *ibid.*, 22 July 1966.
26. *Daily Graphic*, 14 and 19 January 1967.
27. *ibid.*, 30 January 1968.
28. *ibid.*, 24 June 1967.
29. *Legon Observer*, 12 May 1967.
30. *ibid.*, 11 March 1969.
31. *The Economist* (London), 25 March 1967, p. 1131.

CHAPTER V

1. *The Man on Horseback*, London, Pall Mall Press, 1962, p. 14.
2. *Legon Observer*, 14 April 1967.
3. *Daily Graphic*, 18 April 1966.
4. *ibid.*, 7 April 1967.
5. A. A. Afrifa, *The Ghana Coup*, London, Frank Cass, 1966, pp. 107–8.
6. *Daily Graphic*, 12 July 1967.
7. *Sunday Mirror*, Accra, 27 February 1966.
8. Ministry of Information, *A New Era in Ghana*, Accra, State Publishing Corporation, 1966, p. 8.
9. *ibid.*, pp. 22–3.
10. *ibid.*, p. 20.
11. *Legon Observer*, 17 February 1967.
12. NLC *Decree* 59, 24 June 1966.
13. *Legon Observer*, 17 February 1967.
14. *Daily Graphic*, 21 March 1966.
15. A. K. Ocran, *A Myth is Broken*, Harlow, Longmans, 1969, p. 96.
16. J. M. Lee, *African Armies and Civil Order*, London, Chatto and Windus, 1969, p. 112.
17. NLC *Decree* 183, 27 June 1967.
18. NLC *Decree* 188, 21 July 1967.
19. Biographical details from *Ghana Year Book 1969*, Accra, Graphic Corporation, 1969, pp. 108–84.

20. Biographical details from Ministry of Information, *Towards Civilian Rule in Ghana*, Accra, State Publishing Corporation, 1967, pp. 13–14.
21. *Legon Observer*, 5 July 1968.
22. *ibid.*, 2 August 1968.
23. *West Africa*, 9 November 1968, p. 1330.
24. See Chapter III, pp. 44–5.
25. See Chapter II, pp. 22–3 and 30.
26. *Daily Graphic*, 4 March 1966.
27. *ibid.*, 9 July 1969.

CHAPTER VI

1. *Ghana: The End of an Illusion*, New York, Monthly Review Press, 1966, p. 130.
2. *Reap the Whirlwind*, London, McGibbon and Kee, 1968, p. 438.
3. *Ghana Gazette*, 16 October 1957.
4. D. G. Austin, *Politics in Ghana 1946–60*, London, Oxford University Press, 1964, p. 406.
5. *Report* of the Jiagge Commission on Assets of Specified Persons, Accra, Ghana Publishing Corporation, 1968, p. 90.
6. *ibid.*, pp. 53–90.
7. *White Paper* on the Sowah Report on Assets of Specified Persons, Accra, Ghana Publishing Corporation, 22 March 1968.
8. *West Africa*, 16 August 1969, p. 973.
9. *Operation Cold Chop*, Accra, Ghana Publishing Corporation, 1969, pp. 54–5.
10. *Daily Graphic*, 25 March 1965.
11. The *Report* of the Jiagge Commission provides evidence of this in the Central Region, *op. cit.*, pp. 53–90.
12. Ashanti Lands Act, 1958; Stool Lands (Validation of Legislation) Act, 1959.
13. *Dark Days in Ghana*, London, Lawrence and Wishart, 1968, pp. 55–6.
14. H. S. Jacobs, 'The Myth of the Missing Opposition', unpublished manuscript, University of California, 1965, p. 20. Quoted in B. Fitch and M. Oppenheimer, *Ghana: The End of an Illusion*, New York, Monthly Review Press, 1966, p. 75.
15. For a complete list of results, see *Legon Observer*, 5 September 1969.

16. *Africa's Golden Road*, London, Heinemann, 1965, p. 96.

17. P. Barker, *Operation Cold Chop*, p. 57.

18. *ibid.*, pp. 52–3.

19. *Dark Days in Ghana*, pp. 100–1.

20. *Daily Graphic*, 9 June 1969.

21. *Sunday Mirror*, Accra, 27 February 1966.

22. Ministry of Information, *A New Era in Ghana*, Accra, State Publishing Corporation, 1966, p. 20.

23. *Daily Graphic*, 25 March 1966.

24. Ministry of Information, *op. cit.*, p. 12.

25. See especially D. G. Austin, *op. cit.*, Chapters 5–7.

26. See table on p. 117.

27. *Daily Graphic*, 1 November 1967.

28. C. Kudiabor, 'A New Organisation for Development Planning in Ghana', *Legon Observer*, 5 January 1968.

29. Local Government (Interim Administration) *Decree*, NLC *Decree* 26, 24 March 1966.

30. *Daily Graphic*, 30 March 1966.

31. *ibid.*, 27 June 1966.

32. Local Government (Interim Administration) (Amendment), NLC *Decree* 229, 23 February 1968.

33. Legislative Instrument 540, 1 July 1966.

34. *Report* of the Commission on the Structure and Remuneration of the Public Services in Ghana, Accra, Ghana Publishing Corporation, 1967.

35. *ibid.*, pp. 2–8.

36. White Paper on the Mills–Odoi Commission, *White Paper*, 6/68, Accra, Ghana Publishing Corporation.

37. Organisation of Government Machinery Circular, 3/69, 15 May 1969. After the restoration of civilian rule, a further step was taken in implementing the Mills–Odoi proposals, with the introduction of the Local Administration Bill into Parliament in 1971. See *West Africa*, 3 January 1971, pp. 130–1 and 25 June 1971, p. 717.

38. Mills–Odoi Commission, pp. 2–8.

39. *Legon Observer*, 17 February 1967.

40. *Daily Graphic*, 13 February 1967.

41. *ibid.*, 26 October 1966.

42. *ibid.*, 6 July 1967.

43. *ibid.*, 23 June 1967.

44. *ibid.*, 8 January 1968.

45. *ibid.*, 24 June 1968.
46. *ibid.*, 21 October 1967.
47. *ibid.*, 22 June 1968.
48. *West Africa*, 28 September 1968, pp. 1115 and 1151.
49. *Daily Graphic*, 4 September 1968.
50. *ibid.*, 11 September 1968.
51. *West Africa*, 3 May 1969, p. 493.
52. *Ghanaian Times*, Accra, 29 April 1969.
53. *Daily Graphic*, 28 June 1969.
54. *ibid.*, 30 July 1969.
55. *ibid.*, 22 April 1968.
56. Auditor-General's *Report* for 1966–7, Accra, Ghana Publishing Corporation, 1970, pp. 64–7.
57. *ibid.*, p. 66.

CHAPTER VII

1. *The Man on Horseback*, London, Pall Mall Press, 1962, p. 191.
2. J. J. Johnson (ed.), *The Role of the Military in Underdeveloped Countries*, Princeton, N.J., Princeton University Press, 1962, pp. 232–51.
3. *Daily Graphic*, 28 February 1966.
4. *The Ghana Coup*, London, Frank Cass, 1966, p. 124.
5. *West Africa*, 12 April 1969, p. 405.
6. *Legon Observer*, 14 April 1967.
7. *Daily Graphic*, 30 March 1967.
8. *Legon Observer*, 29 September 1967.
9. *The Military in African Politics*, London, Methuen, 1969, p. 154.
10. See Chapter II.
11. *Daily Graphic*, 9 December 1967.
12. Central Bureau of Statistics, *Economic Survey 1966*, Ministry of Information, Accra, 1967, p. 112.
13. Central Bureau of Statistics, *Economic Survey 1968*, Ministry of Information, Accra, 1969, p. 127.
14. *West Africa*, 26 October 1968, p. 1245.
15. Government *Estimates*, 1966–7, 1967–8, Accra, Ghana Publishing Corporation.
16. *West Africa*, 20 July 1968, p. 848.
17. *Ghana Year Book 1969*, Accra, Graphic Corporation, 1969.
18. *Legon Observer*, 28 February 1969.
19. *West Africa*, 19 April 1969, p. 451.

20. *Daily Graphic*, 8 June 1967.
21. *Ghana Year Book 1969*, Accra, Graphic Corporation, 1969, pp. 27–8.
22. *Legon Observer*, 17 February 1967.
23. *Daily Graphic*, 24 January 1967.
24. NLC *Decree* 229, 5 November 1968.
25. NLC *Decree* 183, 30 June 1967.
26. NLC *Decree* 26, 24 March 1966.
27. NLC *Decree* 229, 23 February 1968.
28. *Sunday Mirror*, Accra, 27 February 1966.
29. NLC *Decree* 59, 24 January 1966.
30. *Daily Graphic*, 23 May 1968.
31. *Legon Observer*, 5 July 1968.
32. *ibid.*, 19 July 1968.
33. NLC *Decree* 229, 5 November 1968.
34. *Report* of the Constitutional Commission, Accra, Ghana Publishing Corporation, 1968, pp. 114–15.
35. NLC *Decree* 223, 29 January 1968.
36. NLC *Decree* 251, 25 June 1968.
37. NLC *Decree* 273, 22 August 1968.
38. *West Africa*, 23 November 1968, p. 1389.
39. *Legon Observer*, 22 November 1968.
40. *West Africa*, 23 November 1968, p. 1389.
41. NLC *Decree* 332, 11 February 1969.
42. NLC *Decree* 345, 28 April 1969.
43. NLC *Decree* 347.
44. R. First, *The Barrel of a Gun*, Harmondsworth, Penguin, 1970, p. 405.
45. Prohibited Organizations, *Decree* 358, 6 June 1969.
46. *West Africa*, 12 April 1969, p. 421.
47. *Constitution of the Republic of Ghana*, Accra, Ghana Publishing Corporation, 1969, pp. 36–47. *Report* of the Constitutional Commission, Appendix E, pp. 50–61.
48. *Ghanaian Times*, 5 and 6 May 1969.
49. NLC *Decree* 345, 28 April 1969.
50. *Daily Graphic*, 20 June 1969; *Constitution of the Republic of Ghana*, p. 58.
51. NLC *Decree* 380, August 1969.
52. See especially *Legon Observer*, 27 August 1969.
53. For an analysis of the election issues and the results, see Dennis Austin's article, 'Caesar's Laurel Crown', *West Africa*, 13 September

1969, pp. 1079–81; his series of specially contributed articles, *ibid.*, 16 August to 20 September 1971; and his book, *Ghana Observed*, London, Frank Cass, forthcoming. The Progress Party won every single seat in the Ashanti, Brong-Ahafo and Central Regions. In Greater Accra, the nine seats were shared between three parties and an independent, but it was only in Gbedemah's own Volta Region that his party gained a majority. Detailed results are given in the *Legon Observer*, 5 September 1969.
54. See Chapters II and III.

CHAPTER VIII

1. Central Bureau of Statistics, *Economic Survey 1966*, Accra, Ministry of Information, 1966, pp. 11–12.
2. S. K. Gaisie, *Dynamics of Population Growth in Ghana*, Demographic Unit, Department of Sociology, University of Ghana, 1969, p. 54.
3. Central Bureau of Statistics, *Economic Survey 1968*, Accra, Ministry of Information, 1968, p. 21.
4. *The Guardian* (London), 24 October 1969.
5. Central Bureau of Statistics, *Economic Survey 1968*, p. 102.
6. *A Myth is Broken*, Harlow, Longmans, 1969, pp. 97–8.
7. *The Ghana Coup*, London, Frank Cass, 1966, p. 119.
8. *In Defence of Politics*, Harmondsworth, Penguin, 1964, pp. 90–1.
9. *Politics in Ghana 1946–60*, London, Oxford University Press, 1964, p. 47.
10. *ibid.*, p. 417.
11. See especially the Apaloo *Report* on Kwame Nkrumah's Properties, Accra, Ghana Publishing Corporation, 1966.
12. *Military Institutions and Power in New States*, London, Pall Mall Press, 1964, pp. 141–4.
13. P. C. Lloyd (ed.), *The New Elites of Tropical Africa*, London, Oxford University Press, 1966, p. 9.
14. For both reactions, see *Legon Observer*, 17 February 1967.
15. *A Myth is Broken*, Harlow, Longmans, 1969, p. 94.
16. *Legon Observer*, 5 July 1968.
17. *Daily Graphic*, 7 April 1969.
18. For the full text of the Prime Minister's speech, see *The Star*, Accra, 22 April 1970.
19. *ibid.*

CHAPTER IX

1. S. E. Finer, *The Man on Horseback*, London, Pall Mall Press, 1962, p. 9.
2. W. F. Gutteridge, *The Military in African Politics*, London, Methuen, 1969, p. 143.
3. R. E. Dowse, 'The Military in Political Development', in C. Leys (ed.), *Politics and Change in Developing Countries*, London, Cambridge University Press, 1969, p. 239.
4. *West Africa*, 12 March 1966, pp. 287–8.

Select Bibliography

BOOKS ON GHANAIAN POLITICS AND POLITICAL HISTORY

Afrifa, A. A., *The Ghana Coup*, London, Frank Cass, 1966.

Alexander, H. T., *African Tightrope*, London, Pall Mall Press, 1965.

Apter, D. E., *Ghana in Transition*, New York, Atheneum, 1963.

Armah, A. K., *The Beautyful Ones are not yet Born*, London, Heinemann, 1968.

Austin, D. G., *Ghana Observed*, London, Frank Cass, forthcoming.
   Politics in Ghana 1946–60, London, Oxford University Press, 1964.

Barker, P., *Operation Cold Chop*, Accra, Ghana Publishing Corporation, 1969.

Bennion, F. A. R., *The Constitutional Laws of Ghana*, London, Butterworth, 1962.

Bing, G., *Reap the Whirlwind*, London, McGibbon and Kee, 1968.

Bretton, H., *The Rise and Fall of Kwame Nkrumah*, London, Pall Mall Press, 1966.

Dowse, R. E., *Modernisation in Ghana and in the USSR*, London, Routledge and Kegan Paul, 1969.

Fitch, B. and Oppenheimer, M., *Ghana: the End of an Illusion*, New York, Monthly Review Press, 1966.

Harvey, W. B., *Law and Social Change in Ghana*, London, Oxford University Press, 1966.

Nkrumah, K., *Dark Days in Ghana*, London, Lawrence and Wishart, 1968.
   Ghana (Autobiography), London, Nelson, 1957.
   Voice from Conakry, London, Panaf Publications, 1967.

Ocran, A. K., *A Myth is Broken*, Harlow, Longmans, 1969.

Omari, T. P., *Kwame Nkrumah: The Anatomy of an African Dictatorship*, Accra, Moxon Paperbacks, 1970.

Owusu, M., *The Uses and Abuses of Political Power*, Chicago, Ill., University of Chicago Press, 1970.

Rubin, L. and Murray, P., *The Constitution and Government of Ghana*, London, Sweet and Maxwell, 1961.

Tettegah, J., *Towards Nkrumaism*, Accra, TUC, 1962.

Thompson, W. S., *Ghana's Foreign Policy*, Princeton, N.J., Princeton University Press, 1969.

BOOKS ON AFRICAN POLITICS WITH RELEVANCE TO GHANA

Adu, A. L., *The Civil Service in New African States*, London, Allen and Unwin, 1965.

Almond, G. A. and Coleman, J. S., *The Politics of Developing Areas*, Princeton, N.J., Princeton University Press, 1960.

Armah, K., *Africa's Golden Road*, London, Heinemann, 1965.

Busia, K. A., *Africa in Search of Democracy*, London, Routledge and Kegan Paul, 1967.

Coleman, J. S. and Rosberg, C. G., *Political Parties and National Integration in Tropical Africa*, Berkeley, Calif., University of California Press, 1964.

Hodgkin, T., *African Political Parties*, Harmondsworth, Penguin, 1961.

Leys, C. (ed.), *Politics and Change in Developing Countries*, London, Cambridge University Press, 1969.

Lloyd, P. C. (ed.), *The New Elites of Tropical Africa*, London, Oxford University Press, 1966, p. 9.

Nkrumah, K., *I Speak for Freedom*, London, Heinemann, 1961.
   Africa Must Unite, London, Heinemann, 1963.
   Consciencism, London, Heinemann, 1964.
   Neo-Colonialism: the Last Stage of Imperialism, London, Nelson, 1965.

Miscellaneous

Crick, B., *In Defence of Politics*, Harmondsworth, Penguin, 1964.

Gaisie, S. K., *Dynamics of Population Growth in Ghana*, Accra, Demographic Unit, Dept. of Sociology, University of Ghana, 1969.

BOOKS ON THE MILITARY IN POLITICS

Bienen, H. (ed.), *The Military Intervenes*, New York, Russell Sage Foundation, 1968.

Finer, S. E., *The Man on Horseback*, London, Pall Mall Press, 1962.
   The Politics of Demilitarisation, London, Institute of Commonwealth Studies, University of London, 1966.

First, R., *The Barrel of a Gun*, London, Allen Lane, The Penguin Press, 1970.

Gutteridge, W. F., *Armed Forces in New States*, London, Oxford University Press, 1962.
   The Military in African Politics, London, Methuen, 1969.
   Military Institutions and Power in New States, London, Pall Mall Press, 1964.

Huntington, S. P., *Political Order in Changing Societies*, New Haven, Conn., Yale University Press, 1968.

Janowitz, M., *The Military in the Development of New Nations*, Chicago, Ill., University of Chicago Press, 1968.

Johnson, J. J. (ed.), *The Role of the Military in Underdeveloped Countries*, Princeton, N.J., Princeton University Press, 1962.

Lee, J. M., *African Armies and Civil Order*, London, Chatto and Windus, 1969.

Lefever, E. W., *Spear and Scepter*, Washington, D.C., Brookings Institution, 1970.

Luckham, A. R., *The Nigerian Military*, London, Cambridge University Press, 1971.

Miners, N. J., *The Nigerian Army 1956–1966*, London, Methuen, 1971.

Van Doorn, J. (ed.), *Armed Forces and Society*, The Hague, Mouton, 1968.

Welch, C., *Soldier and State in Africa*, Evanston, Ill., Northwestern University Press, 1970.

ARTICLES

Feit, E., 'Military Coups and Political Development: Some Lessons from Ghana and Nigeria', *World Politics*, January 1968.

Lee, J. M., 'Parliament in Republican Ghana', *Parliamentary Affairs*, Vol. XVI, No. 4, 1963.

Luckham, A. R., 'A Comparative Typology of Civil–Military Relations', *Government and Opposition*, Winter 1971.

Price, R. M., 'Military Officers and Political Leadership: the Ghanaian Case', *Comparative Politics*, April 1971.

'A Theoretical Approach to Military Rule in New States: Reference Group Theory and the Ghanaian Case', *World Politics*, April 1971.

Twumasi, E. Y., 'Ghana's Draft Constitutional Proposals', *Transition*, October 1968.

Ghana Government Publications
REPORTS OF COMMISSIONS AND COMMITTEES OF ENQUIRY
(All issued by the Ghana Publishing Corporation)

1966
Commission of Enquiry into the Affairs of the Erstwhile Publicity Secretariat (Ayeh Commission).

Commission of Enquiry into Kwame Nkrumah's Properties (Apaloo
Commission).

1967

*Commission on the Structure and Remuneration of the Public Services
in Ghana* (Mills–Odoi Commission).
Committee of Enquiry into the Local Purchase of Cocoa (de Graft
Johnson Committee).
Constitutional Commission.
*Commission of Enquiry into Irregularities and Malpractices in the
Granting of Import Licences* (Ollennu Commission).

1968

*Committee of Enquiry into the Delimitations of Functions of University
Institutions* (Busia Committee).
Educational Review Committee (Kwapong Committee).
Commission of Enquiry into the Timber Marketing Board (Blay
Commission).
Commission of Enquiry into Electoral and Local Government Reform
(Siriboe Commission), Parts I and II.
Commissions of Enquiry into the Assets of Specified Persons (Jiagge
and Sowah Commissions), Vol. I.

1969

Commission of Enquiry into Electoral and Local Government Reform
(Siriboe Commission), Part II.
Commissions of Enquiry into the Assets of Specified Persons (Jiagge
Commission, Vol. II; Sowah Commission, Vols. II and III;
Manyo–Plange Commission).

OTHER GOVERNMENT PUBLICATIONS

(All issued by the Ghana Publishing Corporation)
Auditor General's Reports, 1957–.
Budget Statements, 1966–9.
Economic Survey, 1957–.
Estimates, 1957–.
Ghana Gazette, 1957–.
Legislative Instruments, 1957–.
NLC *Decrees*, 1966–9.
Parliamentary Debates 1957–66, 1969–.

1960

Census of Population.
Constitution of the Republic of Ghana.

1966

Ministry of Information, *A New Era in Ghana.*
  The Rebirth of Ghana.

1967

NLC Economic Committee, *Ghana's Economy and Aid Requirements.*
Ministry of Information, *Towards Civilian Rule in Ghana.*

1968

White Paper, *Government Policy on the Promotion of Ghanaian Business Enterprises.*

1969

Constitution of the Republic of Ghana.
Ministry of Information, *Three Years After Liberation.*
  Lest We Forget: Ghana under the NLC.
  Political Party Activities in Ghana Since 1920, Fact Sheet No. 70.
Graphic Corporation, *Ghana Year Book.*
Organisation of Government Machinery Circular, 3/69, 15 May 1969.

NEWSPAPERS

Daily Graphic, Accra.
Evening News, Accra.
Evening Standard, Accra.
Ghanaian Times, Accra.
Legon Observer, University of Ghana, Legon.
Sunday Mirror, Accra.
The Spokesman, Accra.
The Statesman, Accra.
West Africa, London.

PERIODICALS

All England Law Reports, London.
Comparative Politics, Chicago, Ill.
Government and Opposition, London.
Parliamentary Affairs, London.
Transition, Kampala and Accra.
West Africa, London.
World Politics, Princeton, N.J.

Index